HAVING IT ALL/
HAVING ENOUGH

HAVING IT ALL/ HAVING ENOUGH

How to Create a Career/Family Balance That Works for You

Deborah Lee, Ph.D.

with

Cary Martin Zellerbach, Chris Essex,
Leah Potts Fisher, Barney Olmsted

amacom

American Management Association

New York • Atlanta • Boston • Chicago • Kansas City • San Francisco • Washington, D.C.
Brussels • Mexico City • Tokyo • Toronto

This book is available at a special
discount when ordered in bulk quantities.
For information, contact Special Sales Department,
AMACOM, a division of American Management Association,
1601 Broadway, New York, NY 10019.

This publication is designed to provide accurate and authoritative information in
regard to the subject matter covered. It is sold with the understanding that the
publisher is not engaged in rendering legal, accounting, or other professional
service. If legal advice or other expert assistance is required, the services of a
competent professional person should be sought.

Library of Congress Cataloging-in-Publication Data

Lee, Deborah.
    Having it all/having enough : how to create a career/family
    balance that works for you / Deborah Lee ; with Cary Zellerbach . . .
    [et al.].
        p.   cm.
    Includes bibliographical references and index.
    ISBN 0-8144-0345-X (hardcover)
    1. Work and family.   I. Title.
    HD4904.25.L44   1996   96-36242
    331.2—dc20   CIP

Printing number

10 9 8 7 6 5 4 3 2

Contents

Preface

I understand that in most of the natural world of the United
States, both parents work full-time at inflexible jobs. But I don't
know how any of them does it, ever. When do they go to the
doctor? When do they do the laundry? When do they buy the
food? When do they cook the food? Although most of the people
I know do it, I don't understand how they do it, even for one
week. I just barely understand how I do it. To me, it's like trying
to put 150,000 pounds of molasses into a quart bottle.

—Alice, single, psychologist who works
full time at home, one child, age 16

First comes an admission: The author of this book continues to
have a hard time balancing work and family in her own life.

Next, the topic is deep and wide. It's as though someone lifted
a rock and discovered the whole world beneath it. Among the topics that crawl out are sex roles, workaholism, the United States and
the world economy, postpartum responses, the history of the family, American political and social attitudes toward children, self-
discovery, female and male biology, and child development.

Finally, this topic is laden with guilt, especially for women. So
many parents find it impossible to balance work and family, no
matter how hard they try, that almost any book runs the risk of
inadvertently increasing their sense of personal inadequacy.

By work, I mean activities through which individuals contribute
to the larger society and that provide them with economic support.
By family, I mean a group of people who care for one another in a
sustaining way. All of the families described in this book include children who are living with one or both of their parents.

I interviewed forty-seven people who are relatively satisfied
with at least some dimensions of the balance between their work
and family lives. Some work full time, some care for their children

full time; most have found ways to combine both roles. All have a place to live and some source of income, and most are economically comfortable. Some are married, some single.

I wanted to find out what these people share: the essential elements, internal and external, that help them create and maintain a good balance for themselves and for their families. It became clear as I talked to them that these parents were making adjustments in their lives, and not just once but many times, as their children grew, as they matured, as their careers and job skills changed, as new physical and emotional needs emerged. Flexibility was key.

I also interviewed nine people who work with parents, children, and/or employers and who in different ways help people to create more balanced lives.

Their Limits, Our Limits

The stories of the parents who talked with me are as much about limits as possibilities. This book too has its limits.

First, although I have included some of the parents' frustrations as they attempt to balance work and family, I focused primarily on what works for them. Their stories do not represent the complete range of work-family problems, but they do illuminate circumstances and strategies that help to create solutions.

Second, most of the people I interviewed have economic options. All are in families in which at least one parent is employed, and only two have faced forced unemployment. Their financial situations will be familiar to many readers, but they don't represent the hundreds of thousands of low-income families who also are attempting to balance work and family. If this more economically stable group finds the balancing difficult, how doubly challenging it is for those with fewer economic resources.

Third, this book is about how parents balance work, home life, and child rearing. It doesn't address people's need to care for aging parents and other relatives, an issue of growing concern. Today, about 33 million people in the United States are over age 65, and by the year 2030, this population is expected to reach 70 million. Many experts predict that our need to care for aging parents will powerfully affect employees and employers during the next ten years. Although the specific issues of balancing work and elder care are beyond the scope of the book, overlap is assumed in many areas.

Finally, the author hasn't solved this riddle, either personally or theoretically. I, too, am in the process of balancing and learning about balance. This book describes what I have learned so far about the journey that some people, myself included, are undertaking.

What Follows

As I listened to the stories I heard from the people I interviewed, it became clear that there were a few key themes about what enabled them to create balance. I call these the Building Blocks, and they are explored in Chapters 2 through 5. Chapters 6 through 9 describe specific skills in creating balance and are more practical expressions of the Building Blocks. Chapter 10 is a vision of what lies beyond balance.

Acknowledgments

This book has been a labor of love, to which many people contributed. Cary and John Zellerbach are the book's parents. The book was their inspiration, and they have supported it through its development. Cary has edited the entire book several times and contributed writing, suggestions, insight, and experience.

The Zellerbach Family Fund commissioned and supported this book. It has also, for many years, helped me to balance work and family and to work in a way that expresses my dreams. Former Executive Director Edward Nathan has been a treasured friend and source of inspiration since 1979. He gave crucial guidance to this book in many ways, including when he told me to "just go talk to people." The current executive director, Katherine Armstrong, and members of the board of directors have also provided crucial support.

The people who were interviewed for this book are contributing authors. I really had little idea how to proceed until I talked to them. The book grew from their stories. Their examples, as they continue to seek and create balance, are inspiring to me. I am extremely grateful to them for sharing their scarce time and abundant insights.

Thanks to Barney Olmsted, codirector of New Ways to Work, who worked with me on this book from its inception and provided knowledge, encouragement, and balance. Thanks also to Suzanne Smith, the other codirector, who provided, through New Ways to Work, a home for me and the book. She also managed many crucial details.

Thanks to chapter authors Chris Essex and Leah Potts Fisher, of The Center for Work and the Family. Their work over many years in this field greatly increased my understanding and perspective. Thanks also to everyone in the Work-Family Study Group, which they organized. I have participated in this group throughout the writing of the book and have received lots of ideas and inspiration from its members.

Marjorie Beggs of the San Francisco Study Center was the book's first editor. She took a large, unwieldy manuscript and made it manageable. Chris Desser and Linda Artel also contributed crucial editing assistance. Linda Marks opened her home and library. Thanks to Blue Mountain Center for supporting me in the final editing days.

Thanks to my editor at AMACOM, Mary Glenn, who has an invaluable combination of clarity, appreciation, optimism, and organization. This particular blend of traits is exactly what I need. Thanks also to Barbara Horowitz and Carole Berglie.

All of my thanks go to my parents, Richard and Virginia, who taught me, by example, that the most important ingredient in balancing work and family, and anything else, is love. Thanks to my mother, who combined working and taking care of us with such grace that I am in awe of her for making it look so easy. I am thankful for her encouragement, through her belief in me and by her own example. Thanks to my father, who taught me, among other things, that "most of the world's problems could be solved by communication" and that growth, change, and evolving intimacy continue throughout life. Thanks to my brothers, Richard and Peter, who are such loving fathers and who have always shared my adventures. All of them have given me invaluable help and support in my parenting of Logan.

Thanks to my support system, then (when Logan was little) and now. They made being a parent possible and fun. Thanks especially to Joan, Kirk, Deborah, David, Vidya, Ruth, Fred, Linda, Dale, Deva, Barbara, Judith, Sally, Brooks, Jeanne, Judy, Stacey, Susan, Devaki, Ana, Beth, Bobbi, and Phyllis.

Thanks to my partner, Bob, for abundant love, for being such a great father, for bringing balance to my life, and for hanging in there with me through this project and everything else.

Thanks to my stepson, Jake, for his good humor and laughter, which lightened the way.

Thanks to my son, Logan, for bringing me so much light and joy, for inspiring me to try to balance work and family, and for many of the best things I have learned since he came into my life. When he was born, I thought it couldn't get any better. I was wrong. I thank him for the gift of a truthful relationship.

Cast of Characters

Parents

Alice
Single
One child, age 16
Works full time at home office. Psychologist, consultant.
Child in full-time child care from age 18 months.

Andrea
Single
One child, age 3
Works full time in family commercial real estate business, which she co-owns.
Child is cared for in her office by a paid child care worker and by Andrea.

Anita
Married
Three children, ages 33, 37, and 39
Works full time as codirector of a nonprofit organization.
Cared for children full-time when they were young.

Bill
Married
Three children, ages 4, 12, and 17
Works part time as a salesperson; frequently works from home.
Wife works full time.

Bob
Single
One child, age 17
Works full time from home; owns his own trucking business.
Joint custody; shares parenting equally.

Minimal child care; arranges schedule to care for child when he
   has him.

Catherine
Single
Three children, ages 8, 11, and 14
Works full time as an investment consultant.
Child care centers.

Craig
Married
Two children, ages 2 and 4
Works full time as a university administrator.
Wife works full time at home office.
Full-time child care at home.

Dale
Single
Two children, ages 15 and 16
Artist who works full time as a landscaper, gardener, and tree sur-
   geon.
Various child care arrangements.

Dan
Married to Karin
Four children, ages 11, 15, 22, and 24
Works full time as a college administrator.
Wife works part time.
No formal child care; some exchanges with other families.

Dave
Married
Three children, ages 6, 11, and 13
Worked 60 percent time (forty hours a week); now back to full time
   (sixty-five or more hours a week).

Diana
Married
Two children, ages 4 and 6
Works part time as a psychotherapist.
Husband works full time from a home office.
No early child care; nursery school, shared arrangements.

Elena
Married
Two children, ages 9 months and 3
Works full time as an administrative assistant.
Husband works full time away from home.
Sister-in-law does child care in her home.

Elizabeth
Married to Fred
Two children, ages 5 and 10
Works full time as the director of a mental health organization.
Husband works full time.
Family day care with first child; at-home child care, shared with
    another family, with second child; after-school care.

Fred
Married to Elizabeth
Two children, ages 5 and 10
Works full time as a city planning consultant.
Family day care with first child; at-home child care, shared with
    another family, with second child; after-school care.

Gary
Married to Jayne
Two children, ages 2 and 4
Works full time as television journalist.
Wife works 80 percent time.
Had full-time child care in the home but gave it up; later, part-time
    nursery school.

Isabel
Single
Three children, ages 7, 19, and 21
Works full time as perinatal health care worker.
Divorced; shares parenting of 7-year-old with ex-husband.
No child care for two older children; variety of child care for
    youngest.

Janice
Single
One child, age 1
Administrator of a mental health program.

Hired child care worker to care for child at office for six months, then took one year to care for child at home. Plans to return to work full time beginning second year.

Jayne
Married to Gary
Two children, ages 2 and 4
Journalist, works 80 percent time.
Husband works full time.
Had full-time child care in the home but gave it up; later, part-time nursery school.

Jean
Married
One child, age 9
Self-employed as a career counselor; does some work from home.
Husband works full time.
Variety of child care and shared-care arrangements.

Joe
Married to Julie
Two children, ages 5 and 8
Works full time managing real estate investments.
Wife has worked a variety of schedules.
Full-time child care at home.

Judith
Married
Two children, ages 11 and 13
Works 75 percent time as a psychotherapist.
Husband works full time.
Part-time child care in the home.

Julie
Married to Joe
Two children, ages 5 and 8
Investment manager, has worked a variety of schedules: full time until oldest child was 6 years old; 80 percent time for one year; 60 percent time for one and a half years; currently full-time compensation with a flexible schedule.
Full-time child care in the home.

Julio
Married to Rose
One child, age 3
Cares for child full time.
Wife works full time.
No child care.

Karin
Married to Dan
Two children, ages 11 and 15; two stepchildren, ages 22 and 24
Works part time as a psychiatric nurse.
Husband works full time.
No formal child care; some exchanges with other families.

Karl
Married to Wendy
One child, age 2
Works full time.
Wife works full time.
Full-time child care center at wife's work site.

Kate
Married
Two children, ages 3 and 6
Works full time as a supervisor for a public utilities agency.
Husband works full time, away from home, with much travel.
Full-time child care in the home; after-school care.

Kristin
Married
Two children, ages 3 months and 20 months
Cares for children full time.
Husband runs business full time from home.
Full-time child care in the home.

Laura
Married
Three children, ages 2, 4, and 8
Cares for children full time; does writing and consulting from
    home.
Husband works full time.
Supplemental child care in the home.

Lena
Married
One child, age 3
Works part time as a consultant; just quit full-time job as health
  care executive to have more time with child.
Husband works full time.
Child care center.

Leslie
Married
One child, age 12
Works twenty hours a week as education coordinator of a parent
  support organization.
Husband works full time.
No child care.

Linda
Single
One child, age 17
Works full time as an administrative nurse in a health care organi-
  zation.
Child care center during preschool years; after-school care.

Lisa
Married to Ray
One child, age 3
Works full time as bookkeeper in an auto parts store.
Husband cares for child at home full time.
No child care.

Marjorie
Married
Three grown children
Founder and past director of several nonprofit organizations; cur-
  rently works part time as director of nonprofit organization.
Husband works full time.
Occasional supplemental child care when children were young.

Marty
Single
Two children, ages 12 and 17
Works full time as a consultant and teacher.
Joint custody; shares parenting equally.

Matt
Single
Two children, ages 8 and 11
Works full time in sales for a computer firm.
Joint custody; shares parenting equally.
Brief period of child care; mainly parents care for children.

Patricia
Married
Two children, ages 9 and 15
Works full time in community affairs for a large corporation.
Husband works full time.
Brought first child to work with her for first year; otherwise, full-
time child care in centers and family day care.

Polly
Married to Tom
One child, age 2
Works 24 hours a week as a scientist.
Husband works 30 hours a week.
No child care except for a brief, unsuccessful attempt.

Ray
Married to Lisa
One child, age 3
Artist; currently working occasionally; cares full time for child.
No child care.

Richard
Married
Two children, a newborn infant and age 4
Works full time at home as a consultant.
Wife works full time.
Baby in child care; 4-year-old in after-school care.

Rose
Married to Julio
One child, age 3
Works full time for the navy.
Husband cares for child full time.
No child care.

Sharon
Single

One child, age 16
Works full time as a college professor.
Various child care arrangements.

Sherrie
Married
One child, age 2
Cares for child full time and works part time as an administrator of
    a mental health task force; works at home or takes child to work.
Husband works full time.
No child care.

Suzanna
Married
One child, age 6
Works full time at a home office; owns a parent education business.
Husband works full time.
Mothers' play group together with various part-time and share-
    care arrangements.

Tom
Married to Polly
One child, age 2
Works thirty hours a week as a computer software designer.
Wife works part time.
No child care except for a brief, unsuccessful attempt.

Virginia
Married
Three children, ages 42, 44, and 45
Retired; worked full time as a teacher of deaf children.
Husband retired, worked full time.
No child care except after-school with neighbor for youngest child.
    Directed nursery school that children attended.

Wendy
Married to Karl
One child, age 2
Works full time as a projects manager for utility company.
Husband works full time.
Full-time child care center at her work site.

Work-Family Advocates

Linda Artel
Work-family consultant
Berkeley, California

Judy David
One Small Step
United Way
San Francisco

Chris Essex
The Center for Work and the
    Family
Berkeley, California

Leah Fisher
The Center for Work and the
    Family
Berkeley, California

Charles Harris
Psychotherapist, private practice
San Francisco

Tanya Nathan
Corporate child care specialist
The Children's Council of San
    Francisco
San Francisco

Jeree Pawl
Infant-Parent Program
University of California
San Francisco

Ethel Seiderman
Parent Services Project
Fairfax, California

Byron Siegel
Children's Services
University of California
San Francisco

HAVING IT ALL/ HAVING ENOUGH

1

Basic Assumptions

Women walk around thinking that somehow we ought to be able to pull this off—work, partner, family, and self. Even though women have tried to dispel the myth, people get isolated and think, "If I just did it better, I could do it." It's a big myth. The kind of tasks people are trying to do with work and family—it's just impossible.

—Diana, married, part-time psychotherapist, two children, ages 4 and 6

Work and family are both areas of life to which people bring important values and assumptions. Although I wanted to reflect the diverse values and priorities of the people interviewed, I certainly bring to the project my own guiding principles and assumptions. These undoubtedly affected what I asked and what I learned.

Balance Is Both a Personal and a Social Issue

I assume that the challenge of balancing work and family involves individuals and society as a whole. Many solutions must be social or structural: family leave, supportive and affordable child care, schools that welcome parents, workplace supervisors who encourage employees to take time for family responsibilities, executives whose policies enable middle managers to support employees, flexible work options, supportive partners who share equally in work and family responsibilities, child-friendly communities, and biological or friendship-based extended families. All of these elements make an overwhelming difference in how successfully an individual can balance work and family.

In my view, parenting responsibility goes beyond the child's parents to encompass individuals and society, a perspective that is unusual in the United States but is widely accepted in other countries. The American view of individual parents as solely responsible for raising children contributes enormously to the lack of family supports at the workplace. That attitude, which exaggerates the importance of privacy and individualism, must be challenged.

There is no substitute for structural, social supports. Regardless of how early we get up in the morning, how well we manage our time, how clear we are in setting our priorities—in other words, no matter how hard we try—we cannot entirely make up for the lack of societal supports for parenting and for balancing. Well-meaning advice about balancing work and family, including this book, can add to parents' guilt by implying that some magic approach, attitude, or strategy can miraculously make the seemingly impossible possible. Without taking into account social factors, parents, especially mothers, often feel that they can't meet their own goals and standards, as either parents or workers.

A more realistic approach acknowledges that too much is too much. We can't be in more than one place at the same time or do more than one thing at the same time, despite appearances and our best efforts. We can't be more than human, and we suffer hugely if we try to be.

On the other hand, we have no intention of suffering passively while we await social changes. Our individual and collective efforts make a great difference in the quality of our lives. There are situations that we can't fix by ourselves, but we can make choices and take action to make our own and our families' lives as balanced as possible. It is through the sum total of our individual efforts that we collectively change our world. We make these changes one step at a time, each in our own way, together and separately.

Many Ways Exist to Balance Work and Family

Our interviews with parents in a variety of work and family situations demonstrate that there is no single right way to create balance. Each individual and each family need to find a unique, and evolving, solution to work-family dilemmas.

There are, however, a few essential truths:

- ▫ Mothers, not fathers, give birth and nurse infants.
- ▫ A baby needs close, regular, extended contact with people who adore him or her, preferably one or both parents.
- ▫ Every family needs a source of income and a way to care for dependent family members.
- ▫ Parents need a baseline of calm and time in order to be able to be empathic to their children.
- ▫ There are only twenty-four hours in a day.
- ▫ It takes a community to raise a child.
- ▫ Adults and children can flourish in a variety of family arrangements provided there is sufficient support.
- ▫ Children need quality and quantity time with their parents and with other people who love them.

We are a diverse nation of individuals with wide-ranging cultural backgrounds and values. This diversity is a blessing when we consider the issue of balancing work and family. We can, for example, learn a lot from refugees and immigrants who culturally tend to view family and community as priorities in ways that are almost unimaginable to many in the United States. For example, all of the Asian parents interviewed for this book relied extensively on the support of the child's grandparents and other members of their extended families. African-American families also have a rich tradition of caring for one another's children and supporting each other. In many countries, the spheres of adults and children are not separate as they are in the United States, and it is not uncommon to encounter young children being cared for in places of business.

The workforce too is becoming increasingly diverse. Places of business have to acknowledge and accommodate themselves to the differences in their employees' needs and priorities that stem from their various cultures, ages, and family situations. Not everyone in the workplace is involved in raising young children, but all people live within some kind of family or community that at various points in their lives demands their attention.

Being a Parent Is a Primary, Constant Responsibility and Privilege

In searching for balance between work and family life, a parent's primary responsibility is to the child because the child depends on the parent for survival and well-being. When you're caring for a dependent child, all the parts of your life—work, self-development, marriage or partnership, other family, friendships, community life—must support your ability to care for and love your child. The art is to work with those elements to strengthen your parenting. Parents also have the fundamental responsibility of providing for the family financially. Obviously in two-parent families, the partners can divide these responsibilities in a number of ways; single parents must find a way to fulfill both. But whether a family is headed by one or two parents, all families need additional support from extended family and community to accomplish both tasks.

Bob, who runs a small business and is the single parent of a 17-year-old son, describes his efforts to make spending time with his son a priority: "I chose jobs that allowed me to arrange my hours according to the needs of fatherhood. I continue to balance because it's a priority. Those things that you make priorities, you find a way. I'm glad I made my son a priority. The time that you spend raising a kid is precious time. You don't have a second shot at it."

Being a Parent Is Extremely Challenging

Most of the parents interviewed, no matter how much they loved their children and how intensely they valued parenting, found aspects of parenting to be very difficult. A number of the parents said that caring for their children was much more challenging for them than working.

Kristin, a lawyer and married mother of two children under 2 years old, cares for them at home with help, while her husband runs his business from home. She describes her challenges in these words:

> I have felt more pressure taking care of these kids than at any time in my legal profession. I have been involved in some major, major deals, including the selling of Fortune 100 companies, where at four in the morning the deal

seems to be falling through and I've had to find a solution by eight o'clock in the morning. And I've done that. I don't know why that was so much easier. I guess in a way at work I had to tell myself that I was an actor playing a certain role, whereas when I'm at home I'm not playing. I am affecting lives, and I cannot break away from it.

Another parent, Joe, married, the head of a real estate investment firm, and father of two children, ages 5 and 8, observes, "Being a parent enables one to have an impact on another individual's life. What is most difficult is that little kids are little kids. Whatever good intentions parents have, at some point the child is not receptive. When you're tired, they take you to the edge. It is hard at the edge to be philosophical and balanced. It is very hard. It takes a lot of energy to get through a day."

Lisa works as a bookkeeper in an auto parts store while her husband, an artist, cares for their 3-year-old son at home. She told us, "After six weeks, my maternity leave was up and I went back to work. I felt guilty for leaving, but it didn't last long because I felt comfortable that my husband was there with my son. I realized that it was much easier to go to work than to take care of a child."

The essential challenges of parenting are compounded when combined with employment. "One of the worst parts used to be when we both would walk into the house exhausted at 5:30," recalls Gary, a television journalist who works full time while his wife, Jayne, a newspaper journalist, works 80 percent time. Their sons are 2 and 4 years old. "There are two little boys who want your soul. You're trying to take care of them, handle the phone, cook. You eat. Get them into bed at 8:30. Then we would lie on the couch staring at each other. It was the same frantic scene in the mornings. Get up, get out. The old ways, the old schedule didn't work." Gary was able to change his work schedule so that each parent had quality time alone and quality time with the children, a situation that relieved the tension for everyone.

There Is Little Social Support for Parenting

American society gives lip service to the importance and difficulty of quality parenting but in practice does not give priority to the care of children. The economic sacrifices required for most parents to stay home to care for their children, low pay to child care workers and teachers, lack of workplace supports for family life and responsibilities: All these make parenting difficult.

Dr. Jeree Pawl, director of the Infant-Parent Program at the University of California, San Francisco, describes the effects of this lack of support, based on her extensive experience working with infants and their parents from all walks of life. "We act as if raising children is not important and that the only important thing for women to do is to join men," she notes. "There is no recognition that helping to shape a human being is vitally important. The role of being home with children is not considered working because one is not considered to be producing anything. It is not counted in the gross national product. Yet when one tries to pay for care, even at an inadequate level, one can't afford it."

To change this situation, individuals must assert that parenting is valuable and insist that this value be expressed at all levels of society. It's useful to act as though the world around us has the capacity for appreciating and supporting children and families, even if appearances are not always encouraging.

Julie, an investment manager who is married to Joe, has worked a variety of schedules since her children, now ages 5 and 8, were born; she now works 80 percent time. "I had to educate them at work about my reality," she says. "I had to communicate to them my feelings of conflict and how deeply they affected me."

According to Dr. Pawl, "There needs to be a lessening of demands on young people in terms of careers that preclude time and energy available to their families. Nine to five is one thing. But today there are often expectations that people will work eighteen to twenty hours a day, six days a week. A person might as well be poverty stricken and hold down four jobs for the time they have to put into these time-intensive careers. We need a quality of life track, not a mommy track—an alternate structure. Both parents are feeling the need to be with their children."

It Is Essential to Choose to Be a Parent

With or without structural supports, parents need to embrace their role as parent, whether the pregnancy is planned or a surprise, whether the baby is greeted with joy or ambivalence, no matter the number of parents in the home. Choosing to be a parent helps us carry out the difficult tasks of parenting without rancor. An exhausted single parent probably doesn't want to get up one more time in the middle of the night to change the baby's diapers when he has to go to work the next day, but if he chooses to be a parent, to make that deeper commitment, then he can find a reason to get up and change the baby's diapers anyway.

This sense of choosing helps us to balance work and family in a number of ways. It can help us to make choices that support our ability to parent, even if those choices are not valued or understood by much of surrounding society. Whether this choice means that one parent will stay home for several years to care for the child, that the parent will walk out of the office at 5:00 P.M. enduring stares of disapproval from people without children who are "free" to stay until 7 P.M., or the parent will return to work because he or she feels that this decision is in the best overall interest of the family, it is essential to know that our choices reflect our parental responsibility as a high priority.

Choosing to be a parent also helps us to endure situations we may not have chosen—for example, if we have to go back to work before we are ready or work longer hours than we wish. Being able to assert, "I choose to have this child, to be a parent to this child, to do the best I can, although conditions in the world, at my job, in my life are not perfect," enables us to have a positive attitude, take responsibility, advocate for ourselves and for our families, and provide a good example to our children about their responsibility for their own lives.

Children Need and Deserve Happy Parents

Research confirms that it takes happy, fulfilled, healthy parents who understand and try to meet their own needs to raise happy, fulfilled, healthy children. As parents, we can't respond to our children's needs, or anyone else's for that matter, until we can identify and respond to our own needs. At the same time, we have to learn to separate our subjective reality from our children's. We have to be clear about who feels what, who needs what, and whose needs have priority at any given moment.

We also have to love the child, listen deeply to the child's needs, and often act on behalf of the child, regardless of our preferences. We have to recognize that the child is dependent on us to respond to her or his needs for a limited period of time: infancy and childhood. It is essential that we as parents fully embrace this responsibility. This process can't occur in an atmosphere of self-denial or martyrdom. We can't pretend that it's possible, in any relationship, to meet the needs of one person and ignore the needs of another.

This book assumes that there is enough love, time, and attention to go around if everyone gets involved and if families receive necessary social support. It rejects the idea that decisions about balancing work and family can be made in a spirit of denial, where the needs of one family member are addressed at the expense of another's.

Among other skills, this approach requires us to distinguish between deep, core needs and short-term, immediate preferences or impulses. For example, under too much stress, we may get to the point where we want to run away from our family, to be free and indulge ourselves. But with effort, even in a state of exhaustion, we can recognize that our deeper need is to be responsible to our children and to ourselves and that we can't really do one without the other. If we are responsive to all of these needs, we will have to find a way to get a little time for ourselves, even if we feel guilty or face criticism. We will also have to find time to be with our children and other family members. This essential sorting requires honesty, courage, and resourcefulness. It also requires us to view children as separate individuals rather than extensions of us. Finally, it requires support from the community, from our workplaces, and from policymakers.

Affirm the Joy in Parenting

Parenting can be a vastly satisfying experience. For many, it is one way to achieve deep happiness. This feeling cannot be forced or faked, but it can be cultivated in many ways. Allowing ourselves to experience and acknowledge the joys of parenting can help us to balance work and family.

"I'm ecstatic about being a mother. I have been from the beginning," explains Jean, who has a 9-year-old son, is married, and works part time at home as a consultant and career counselor. "It's great to have a kid, to watch him grow, take care of him. I see that the world is wonderful, original, when I'm with him."

Says Fred, who is married and actively involved in the care of his two children—a 5-year-old daughter and 10-year-old son— "My relationships with them are like no others in the world—seeing two people in a different way, knowing them intimately, and knowing things about them and what's going on with them that I'll probably never know about anybody else."

Laura is married and cares for her three young sons, ages 2, 4, and 8, full time, with paid help, while working occasionally as a writer and consultant. She told us, "I feel profoundly blessed by my children. I just think they made me a human being. Being with my children is a deeply humbling and wonderful experience, and for me it's a journey of self-discovery that is equal to no other."

"The wonders come every day," observes Gary. "To see a child's brain begin to develop and to see the unfolding of that logic process and rationale fills you with love, joy, pride. It's so terrific." Gary picks up his sons from school every day and cares for them during the afternoons.

Satisfying Work Contributes to Family Life

People have the capacity to derive great joy, satisfaction, and growth from their work, and this pleasure and learning can contribute positively to their family life. Of course, not everyone loves his or her work, nor does everyone work primarily for satisfaction. Many people work for economic survival, whether or not they are also lucky enough to have work they enjoy. Work can serve important functions and meets significant needs, whether or not people actually love their work. In our interviews, many parents emphasized that having work that they love, or at least value, contributes positively to creating good work-family balance.

Fred and his wife, Elizabeth, both work full time, she as director of a mental health organization and he in a city planning consulting firm. "My son is just starting to get some grasp of what I do now and make reference to it," Fred told us. "He has said to me, 'You're lucky you like what you do.' I know it's true. If I'm happy with what I'm doing then I'm happier at home too. I've certainly had periods where I have not been happy with work. The family is solace, but in terms of bringing some positive energy to the family, it definitely helps to be happy with what you're doing."

Isabel is a single mother of three children, ages 7, 19, and 21. She works full time as a perinatal health care worker and shares parenting the youngest child with her ex-husband. "I don't think I would like to be home full time," she says. "I just have this energy. Part of me wants to be an independent woman. I want a profession. I want to be out in the world and see what's going on. I've always been that way. Even when I was home with my girls, I was never really home. I was involved with all these volunteer activities, involved with the neighbors, doing something. Now I'm getting paid for it. Loving my work is one of the main things that helps me balance work and family. My heart and soul are in it."

Anita is the codirector of a nonprofit organization, and the married mother of three grown children. According to her, "As my children have gotten to be adults, our relationship has changed from a parent-child to an adult-adult relationship. I think one of the things that has enabled that to happen has been the fact that I've had work that I cared about. I haven't had to hang onto my old family roles as a way of legitimizing myself and as part of my identity. I get other identity strengths, and that's been very helpful."

Patricia, mother of two children ages 9 and 15, is married and directs a community affairs program for a large corporation. She reflects, "It helps to be in a position where you feel you have some control in regard to your work." Parents who lack this power—for example, who can't adjust their work schedule so they can pick up their baby from child care or stay home with a sick child—are likely to become resentful about the work itself and whoever is blocking their need for more flexibility. In fact, it's probably impossible to create any significant work-family balance without having the ability to influence our working conditions.

Combining Roles Can Contribute to Health

Since so many people find joy and fulfillment from work and from parenting, it is not surprising that combining work and child rearing is what many parents want. They also want to find a sane way to develop and express various dimensions of themselves as they fulfill their responsibilities. These wishes are consistent with the results of research. In her extensive 1991 survey of the literature on women and employment, Faye Crosby documented a substantial and consistent body of studies that overwhelmingly indicate that women who combine roles have less depression and greater self-esteem and life satisfaction than women who play fewer roles.[1]

Catherine, a single parent with three children, ages 8, 11, and 14, works full time as an investment consultant. She frames her ideas about family and career using language from the work she loves: "Having both work and family is a plus, a diversification of risks. Portfolio theory says you should diversify your risks so that if things don't go well in one area, it doesn't wipe you out. And that's what life is. I do think working mothers are lucky, because they are naturally diversified in having both family and work to care about."

Dale, another single parent with two children, ages 15 and 16, who works as a landscape gardener, also spoke eloquently of the benefits she derives from combining work and parenting:

> Being away from my children hasn't been all onerous. Working in the field that I really love, meaning landscape and horticulture and environmental science, and its separateness from the constant bombardment of child raising has frequently been really comforting and a balancing agent. It has given me a sense of esteem that I wasn't experiencing in my own home and a sense of progression that I wasn't necessarily seeing as a parent. I think the whole bigger picture of needing to make a good living has given me a kind of determination and fire that I wouldn't have otherwise.

Polly, a scientist, and her husband, Tom, a computer software designer, both work part time so that they can combine professional and family roles and share equally in the care of their 2-year-old daughter. Polly told us why she makes this effort: "I like seeing the whole world. I like the time with Ellen and the time with other adults, the intellectual work. Occasionally the transition is difficult; usually it is not. I just can't imagine not being with her."

Combining Roles Can Be Stressful

The parents we interviewed made it clear that although combining parenting and work roles can be healthy, creative, and growth enhancing, it also can be overwhelmingly stressful, especially when the number and range of demands collide. Sharon, a college professor and single mother of a 16-year-old daughter, described this phenomenon vividly:

> I have a friend who has one child the same age as mine; like me, she is involved in lots of different things. We were both on a committee together that had planned a conference. One of the days of the conference, we both had our daughters there, and they were helping, sort of, and then her daughter had to go over to her high school and my daughter wanted to go with her. My friend was running around saying, "I've got to stop now; I've got to take her over there." I said that since she was the chairperson, I would drive them. I just had to laugh, and I said, "You know, we really need something like a three-corner hat with about eight corners on it. I need a hat that turns, so that I can be clear what role I am in when." I had just shifted from being a member of the committee to being mother, driver. And I think those sort of rough transitions can be long and very weary.

Of course, as Crosby points out, stress also frequently results from factors within one of the roles, such as lack of control over one's work situation, inadequate income, and disproportionate responsibility for home and family.[2] Social factors always come into play. If it were safe in Sharon's community for 16-year-olds to travel by bus and if good public transportation were available, or if their fathers had flexible jobs and were available for more parenting responsibilities, neither mother would have had to stop what she was doing to drive the girls to school.

"A lot of women, especially in these economically difficult times, feel they have to maintain their jobs and have some sort of financial independence," observes Tanya Nathan, corporate child care specialist for The Children's Council of San Francisco, which provides child care referrals to parents and assists corporations in developing supports for the parents among their employees. "There's this incredible pressure to keep your job together, even if things are falling apart in your home life and your child care. It's related to the fact that women's income tends to go down drastically after a divorce, while men's goes up." This kind of "between-role" stress exists on top of "within-role" stress, such as working long hours, meeting deadlines, surviving downsizing at work, or feeling isolated, unappreciated, confused, or bored at home.

Transitions from one role to another can be stressful. Both the career-oriented person who suddenly finds that he wants to spend more time at home once the child is born and the person who thinks she wants to stay at home but then finds the isolation devastating may be equally stressed by the gap between their experiences and their expectations.

Judith, a married psychotherapist with two children, ages 11 and 13, regrets the stress that she experienced by constantly exposing herself to multiple roles:

> I'm sorry that I rushed the children. "Hurry up" must have been their first word. I'm sorry I couldn't let myself match their pace, and yet it would have made me frantically anxious, not knowing that I'd be in the same place ten years later whether I took a break or not. Since I didn't know that at the time, to be slowed down and hanging out in parks with them frightened me too much to do it. But with twenty-twenty hindsight, I wish, more for my sake than for theirs, that I'd had the chance to really be a stay-at-home mom and to sleep when I was tired and eat when I was hungry.

Stress is not necessarily bad, and mastering a stressful situation can produce growth. Alice told us that she has always worked at home and loves doing it, but it has its challenges:

> It was essential when my son was younger, and now that he's a teenager I like being there when he gets home from school, to have a chance to know what he's doing, to know his friends. But still, it's very disruptive. As soon as he gets home, I know I won't be able to do anything that requires concentration. Sometimes I feel that I'll explode

when the multiple demands from different parts of my life happen at once, often all with deadlines. I have to remind myself that I want to be home, that he won't be home forever. I have the rest of my life to shield myself from interruptions. Being disrupted in this way is a great privilege, when I remember.

Balancing Work and Family Involves Both Men and Women

We assume that both men and women need to find a balance between work and family, though they may experience this issue very differently. In contrast to our perspective, the evidence suggests that most women as well as men regard this issue as one that primarily concerns women. Tanya Nathan, who spends much of her time talking to parents struggling with work and family issues, says, "I hate to act like work and home balancing is just a women's issue, because it isn't, but I think the fact is that it's mainly women who are dealing with it. If more men had to compensate because their child was sick or had to take their child to the dentist, there'd be a lot more attention to it. Because it's women who have all these sorts of problems, it becomes a back-seat issue."

Although we assume that issues of work and family affect men and women, we do not assume that they experience these issues in the same ways. As discussed in more detail in Chapter 2, women as a group certainly continue to assume a disproportionate share of the work involved in home and family, regardless of the number of hours they work outside the home. These differences probably reflect historical, social, and biological factors. For example, biological gender differences may affect how parents approach the need to find balance. Gary describes his experience of parenting his son when he was an infant: "When Jason was born, Jayne took five months off. Then I took one month off to stay at home with him. I didn't feel I could care for a child right off the bat. The woman has carried the child for nine months and is more connected at the beginning. After five months, I felt ready. I knew I had skills. It brought me much closer to my child. Jason is more bonded to me than to Jayne. If you care for the child, you can really be part of that imprint time."

Tom is another parent who took on the challenges of caring for an infant. From the time of their daughter's birth, he and his wife both worked part time so that they could share in her care. "Since I couldn't nurse her, it was difficult," he told us. "There were just a few things that worked, but nothing that I knew would work 100 percent. We had her favorite tape, and she liked to go for walks. She never was very fond of the bottle, although she would take it. It wasn't like a cuddling, comforting thing. Overall, I think she was happy. For me, even though it was challenging, it was wonderful just being with her, because if Mom was around she'd look to Mom to nurse. It was very rewarding for me to have her look to me for her needs."

All of the men interviewed for this book take an active role in caring for their children. Although they may be atypical, it is certainly true that both men and women are affected by work-family issues, and it is abundantly apparent that balance cannot be accomplished on any large scale until both men and women are actively engaged in creating balance.

Summing Up

We now turn to the four building blocks that can help us move toward balance in our home and work lives, the negotiations we can undertake to make our work lives more flexible and our relationships with our partners more equitable, how and why to take time for ourselves, and ideas for creating networks to provide essential support and community.

Before plunging in, here's a summary of our assumptions about balancing work and home:

- There are many involved, committed parents of both genders who have found ways to balance work and family. These men and women, and others like them, remind us that it is possible to create a more balanced society.
- Men and women need to share responsibility for balancing work and family. Equal responsibility doesn't require a specific division of labor or arrangement, but it does mean that both partners are responsible for creating arrangements that work for them and the family.

❑ Individuals and families need to create solutions that work for *them*, not measure their solutions against traditional or unconventional gender roles or family constructs.

❑ There's no one balancing solution for all time for any parent or family. Our needs, as parents and as workers, and our children's needs, evolve. Many of us eventually will become responsible for the care of our elderly parents, and increasing numbers of grandparents are assuming primary care for their grandchildren. We may not know what to expect, but it's wise to expect change.

❑ Our institutions must acknowledge and respond to people's development as well as to society's changes. As the workforce includes increasing numbers of women and people of color, the culture and practices of these workplaces must evolve to reflect their values and to enable them to contribute to their full potential. For example, a responsive workplace could give more opportunities to older people, who have completed child rearing and have much to contribute to work, or to adolescents, who have abundant idealism and energy. Perhaps, they could ask less of new parents, who need to focus their energy on their newborns. There are many rewards for a workplace that organizes itself to support the needs of parents: higher morale, lowered absenteeism, reduced turnover, improved recruitment, and, ultimately, a stronger society with happier families and healthier children.

Notes

1. F. J. Crosby, *Juggling* (New York: Free Press, 1991), pp. 15–16, 61–79.
2. Ibid., pp. 41–55.

2

Building Block 1

Identifying and Acting on Our Needs and Priorities

What helps is to be honest with yourself and do a little self-audit from time to time. I started to travel a road, to be very honest with myself, to develop myself into the person I wanted to be. I haven't met all my goals but I sure have tried.

—Joe, married, full-time real estate investment manager, two children, ages 5 and 8

Every individual has different needs and priorities in balancing work and family, and those needs change throughout life. No single solution works for everyone for all times. But knowing what we need and accepting the fact that we need it comprise the first building block in creating work-family balance.

Knowing What We Need

To create the kind of work-family balance we want, we have to know what we need. This observation may seem obvious, but knowing what we want and need is an extremely complicated process for many of us that takes hard work. Identifying our needs depends on how we see ourselves, what choices we believe are appropriate or possible, how much time we have to give to the search, and the extent to which we'll even allow ourselves to address these issues.

In our interviews, many people who were happy with their work-family balance said they engaged in self-examination to determine their own needs and make conscious choices. They considered the relative value of work and family in their lives, and though some gave greater priority to one or the other, all identified living a balanced life as important. Suzanna, who is married, runs her own business from her home, and is the primary caretaker for her 6-year-old son, observes, "I think what is hard is deciding what is important and protecting it." Fred adds, "If I were to pass out advice—not that I've done this—I'd really think about what you want to get out of your life, which is not an easy thing to figure out." Catherine describes another dimension of this challenge: "People can't easily get at what their own expectations are. They don't want to admit it."

Work-family counselor Linda Artel has this advice for parents who are struggling with work and family issues:

> Look at your expectations to see what beliefs, values, and standards you hold about what being a parent and a professional should be. Look at how your life is similar to and different from your parents'. Look for any conflicts in your belief systems. See if there's any old baggage you're dragging around that you can let go of. See if you have any beliefs that are interfering with finding perfectly good solutions now. Maybe your ideas have changed since you had a baby, either forever or temporarily. How can you change your attitudes to help yourself handle work and family?

We can't create a workable arrangement in the world outside ourselves until we're clear about our needs. Inner clarity may not be sufficient to overcome external barriers, but it's an essential precondition. When we can articulate our values and preferences, we are much better able to imagine, and then create, a positive balance.

Tanya Nathan explains how parents' attitudes toward child care often reflect their degree of clarity about work and family issues:

Parents will call and some of them have given themselves enough time to look at various aspects of child care. You can tell that the whole picture is all right for them. They are pretty open to considering new things. They want to spend the time looking around. You know that it is going to work for them, but that's because the other pieces are in place. When we followed up with them, they had found something. They were happy with it, and it was working out, even if there was some juggling and it wasn't working perfectly. Then some other people will call and nothing could work for them. We'll give them fifty or a hundred referrals, and they hate all of them because they are feeling as if things are not working out in their relationship or they are not happy with the amount of time they spend at the job. They'll never be satisfied with the child care.

What are some of the difficulties that keep us from articulating and acting on our own needs? First, it's hard to make the effort if we expect to be discouraged or punished for expressing what we want or if we're convinced we won't be able to act on what we learn about our needs. It might seem pointless to search our soul and decide we need to spend more time with our families if we have a boss who expects us to work twelve-hour days, including Thanksgiving and the day after. It's discouraging to realize that we want to spend significant time with our newborn and ask for paternity leave—assuming the company has a paternity leave policy—if we know that the asking itself labels us as uncommitted to our career and ensures that we'll be passed up for advancing, challenging, creative work or, worse, laid off. What good does it do to decide the kind of child care we want to provide for our children if it doesn't exist at any price, let alone at a price we can afford? We need to know that when we identify and express our needs, there's a chance to get a positive response.

Despite these understandable feelings, it does not follow, if we are in situations that are unresponsive and inflexible, that we shouldn't bother to make the effort to identify and articulate our needs. Being clear about and committed to our bottom line is a necessary precondition for change. The point is to forgive ourselves if we are having a hard time defining our priorities about work and family and understand how hard it is to do this work when we feel we have little or no reason to expect a positive, supportive response.

Although differing widely in their circumstances, our interviewees were very clear about the value of making conscious choices. Sharon says, "It really does help me to have the feeling that all of these were choices that I made. I am able to say that I work in each of the places that I work because I love it, that it is gratifying to me. I chose to have my child, and I chose the time in my life that I was going to have her. There were some things that I didn't choose, but I still made choices around these nonchoices. And I think that is real important."

Sometimes people make this discovery backward—by noticing the results when they denied, or were forced to deny, their own needs. Julie had difficulty moving to a more flexible schedule after her second child was born. She reflects, "People need what they need and will keep trying to get it until they succeed. If they don't get it, it will have repercussions in the sense of feeling anger and resentment. You can't deny what you really need. I didn't know what I really needed until after the baby was born." Her comments also illustrate that learning what you need is an ongoing process that requires the willingness to experiment and to change your sense of who you are in response to new events and perceptions.

Gender-Specific Challenges for Women

Although both men and women face the fear of being rejected for what they truly want, other barriers to identifying needs can break down along gender lines.

Women Are Caught in a Double Bind

Women are affected by conflicting expectations for the roles they play. As workers and as adults, they, like men, are expected to be strong, competent, competitive, articulate, rational, assertive, and tough. As women and as mothers, they are simultaneously expected to be empathic, warm, understanding, patient, sensitive, giving, and self-effacing. To avoid "failure" in one of their roles, many women feel that they must simultaneously work at a job and not work at a job, pick the baby up and let the baby cry, leave at 5:00 P.M. and stay to finish the project, assert themselves and not assert themselves. Clearly it is impossible to fulfill the expectations of both roles simultaneously.[1] This damned-if-you-do, damned-if-you-don't conundrum makes it difficult for a woman to figure out who she really is and what she wants to do. The only solution is for women to reject the social expectations associated with their roles and create their own definitions, standards, and goals.

Some women define and follow their own path with relatively little conflict. "I've never really been ambivalent about work," says Elizabeth, who is married to Fred, has a 5-year-old daughter and a 10-year-old son, and works full time directing a mental health organization. "I've always wanted to work, and sometimes I even don't think it's the right thing to do, but it's the practical thing to do. It's what makes sense. I've always seen myself as a worker, always been excited about the world and how it operates, and wanted to be a part of that."

Sherrie, the married mother of a toddler, who works part time for a mental health advocacy group, is equally unconflicted: "Ideally I'd stay home completely for five years. There's nothing I ever wanted to do in my life besides be a mother. It's easy for me to set my priorities. I enjoy working, and I do a good job. But it's not as important as my personal life—the quality of my relationships."

But many others have to work very hard to recognize their own needs amid the conflicting demands of their different roles and diverse potential. Jayne describes the tug she feels between work and family in this way: "What is my ideal fantasy? As the children get older, they are more fun. I daydream more often about working fewer hours or working from home. But I'm not sure. I like journalism. But sometimes I want to take a year off and just be a mom." She has given herself permission to pay attention to her own needs, though they include conflicting feelings. Feeling ambivalent is progress on the path to breaking out of the double bind.

Women Carry an Unequal Share of Home and Child Responsibilities

Regardless of how much they work outside the home, women usually do most of the child care and housework. The evidence is overwhelming that women carry a disproportionate burden because they have shared the task of supporting the family economically to a far greater degree than men have shared the task of caring for home and children. The result of this disparity is a significant amount of extra work for women, a phenomenon that sociologist Arlie Hochschild of the University of California, Berkeley, terms the "second shift."[2] She calculates that over the course of a year, women work an extra month of twenty-four-hour days.

And no matter how labor is distributed inside and outside the home, most women and most men continue to hold women responsible for carrying the mental load about home and child responsibilities. "Just tell me what you want me to do," says the man who has reached the point where he is willing to "help." This burden makes it difficult for many women to focus on and address their own needs.

Laura describes this phenomenon: "It's not the work. It's not the picking up. It's not the dishes. It's not any of that stuff. Manual labor is nothing—nothing, nothing, nothing—compared to the emotional responsibility, the executive responsibility."

Women usually experience a profound sense of relief when their husbands take on real responsibility for home and children, even if only temporarily. "I went on a business trip and left my husband a list of where our son needed to be when," says Jean. "At the end of ten days he said, 'My life is harder; I work longer days. But your days are more complicated.' He then appreciated what I do because he had done it himself." She felt gratified by this experience, although she retained responsibility for preparing the list.

Expectations vs. the Realities of Motherhood

Many women feel tremendous pressure to deny or downplay the psychological effects of being biologically female. The pressure is a result of the devaluation of the female gender role. This denial, however, often comes to a screeching halt when women become pregnant, give birth, and nurse their infants. It becomes virtually impossible to deny the reality of gender differences in these intense and compelling moments. Giving birth may open women up to a whole new world of needs and experiences. It can be very disconcerting if their experiences don't match their expectations. For example, many women have not been adequately prepared for the consequence of biological attachment to their infants and often are astounded by the intensity of their feelings.

"When I went back to work after Michael was born, I woke up every morning grieving," recalls Julie. "Going back to work at six weeks really made me feel as if someone in the family had died. When my children were born, that whole side of myself was born, too. I had to start all over again with a whole new plan and outlook for my life."

For some women, this experience leads to a profound shift in their understanding of and commitment to their needs. Wendy works full-time as a manager of special projects for a utilities company and shares parenting of her toddler son with her husband, Karl, who also works full-time. "I wish I hadn't gone back to work so soon after he was born. He was 2 months old. I was working at a different company then, and I had made a commitment to go back. I had no idea two months would go so fast. My work was so important to me then—I identified with it—the position, the company. That has changed. I like my job and my employer, but having a child helps me keep work in perspective."

On the other hand, many women we interviewed said they had always assumed they would stop working when they had their children and that the mother role would be primary. Some discovered that staying home as a full-time mother wasn't the fulfilling experience they had envisioned. "When I had a child, I assumed I would stay at home for eighteen years," says Leslie, who is married, has a 12-year-old daughter, and works half-time as education coordinator for a parent support organization. "I felt responsible to be with her, and I enjoyed it. But after six months at home, I found I couldn't sit and play with a baby full time. Then I started working part time."

Other women who planned to continue working found the return easier than they had expected. Lisa returned to full-time work as a bookkeeper when her son was 6 weeks old, leaving him in the care of her husband, Ray. "I've been working since I was as small as I can remember with my dad at the laundry," she told us. "I've always worked. Staying home all of a sudden to be with my son, even for just six weeks, was fun, but I wasn't used to being home for that long. When it was time to get back to work, I was ready to talk and to interact with people."

Some women found creative ways to ease the shock of the transition, from working to parenting or parenting to working. Janice, a single mother who is administrator of a mental health program, brought her infant to work with her for several months to prepare herself for the transition to being home as a full-time mother. Then after this weaning-from-work process, she took a one-year maternity leave.

Fears of Falling Behind in Career Progress

Some women who have fought hard for the opportunity to work, especially in previously male-dominated fields, are afraid of falling behind in their careers if they make home a priority. These fears of sacrificing career advancement are all too often well founded. Overcoming this barrier usually requires a combination of change in circumstances—the option to increase flexibility or reduce work hours without sacrificing career advancement—and in attitude—changing priorities, developing confidence that over time women can realize their goals.

Polly describes the change in her approach to her career after she had her baby: "I had to educate myself. I had certain expectations about what I would be doing to keep current with my profession. That's what everyone else did. I would send careful faxes to my boss about my plans, about when I would return to work. It was a big step to think about not working full time. I was afraid that I would be derailed on my career path. It's not a big issue now. I'll be able to meet my goals. If not, it's not so important."

Mother Guilt

Many mothers feel a pervasive sense of guilt about working out-side the home. This guilt makes it hard for them to define their own needs and goals and commit themselves to fulfilling them. Guilt is a common consequence of the double bind; if a woman strives to fulfill her conflicting role requirements, she is bound to fail at one or the other. Many women, unaware that they are vainly trying to satisfy conflicting demands, blame themselves.

Ethel Seiderman is founder and director of the Parent Services Project, Inc., which develops the capacity of child care centers, early education sites, and schools to create supportive partnerships with parents and other family members. She observes, "It's important for people to get over the hurdle of the guilt, because all the guilt does is keep you trapped."

Our discussions with mothers did not uncover universal guilt among them, but guilt certainly was a challenge for many. Judith describes this dimension of her life:

> I felt guilty every step of the way, and it's meant I've had to work very hard. There's a way in which with both my children I've been a sitting duck for being guilt-induced because they can just smell how guilty I am about everything. I felt terribly guilty about leaving my first child, and yet it truly never entered my conscious mind that I would do anything else. I was a woman with a profession. I would have felt equally guilty leaving my patients. At that point I knew them better than my child.

Women we interviewed who didn't have this burden of guilt tended to accept their limits. Some said they didn't feel guilty because they knew they had no choice but to work. Others felt they wouldn't be very effective if they stayed home full time. Still others believed that their working served their families in ways that extended beyond the economic benefits. Some mothers felt their children were benefiting in unique ways because of the quality of child care they were receiving.

Catherine says, "Maybe I would feel differently if I thought I was the world's greatest expert on how to be with a child, but I don't think I am." Elaborating on this theme, Kate, a married mother of two children, ages 6 and 3, who works full time as a supervisor for a public utilities agency, observes, "I have never once felt any guilt at all about working. I think I would be so unhappy being home and with the children all the time that my children would really suffer. They'd feel it. I'd take my unhappiness out on them somehow."

Most of the women we interviewed who stayed home all or part of the time did not describe any struggle with guilt about not working or about working fewer hours. They detailed other feelings, such as a need to wean themselves from work, having to overcome fears about not advancing in their careers, adjusting to a slower pace, disliking the isolation, or confronting changes in their identities. A possible reason that these women feel stress about not working but not guilt is that mothers are assigned, and take on, responsibility for the well-being of others, particularly their children. If they feel stressed about not working, they are more likely to accept these feelings as their own challenge and less likely to feel that they are neglecting others.

Guilt is tricky and multidimensional. Sometimes it can be a warning response that we're neglecting key people or responsibilities in our lives. In other instances, guilt can be a habitual distracter, a way to deny responsibility for our own needs and feelings. It may be easier to believe we are neglecting our children and feel guilty than to admit how devastated we feel about our separation from them. Or it can be less painful to feel guilty about not being at work than to admit that we would really rather spend some significant time there. Guilt can feel preferable to horror at our own powerlessness to give our children what we want them to have.

Many of our "non-guilt-prone" interviewees emphasized that they were spending significant amounts of time at home with their children, working at their jobs, or both, because they wanted to, not because they felt that choice was essential for their children's well-being. They perceived, and research confirms, that children can flourish in a variety of circumstances. These women made choices not from guilt but because they believed that their needs counted and could be reconciled in a healthy way with the needs of other family members.

Julie found that things got better for her when she cut back her hours at work:

> There are deep feelings I have that my husband just doesn't have. He loves them to death and he's a great father, but when Monday comes, he's had enough. He doesn't have a deep yearning to be at Alexis's ballet class or Michael's baseball practice. I do. It's not out of guilt. It's for the pure

pleasure of it. It's not because I think they're going to be better children. It's just because I really enjoy it. I changed my life because of my needs, not the kids' needs. They were fine. I was the one feeling deprived.

Only by making sure that we're not neglecting ourselves, by being truthful about our own needs, can we be in any position to assess accurately the needs of others in our lives. Too often women reverse the order of this assessment.

Women's Stress

As a group, women experience more stress than men, regardless of whether they're balancing work-family roles and whether they have children. Compared to men, women experience more stress as parents and more stress as workers. But there's no evidence that women who combine roles experience more stress than women who don't.[3] Efforts to identify and ameliorate the real causes of women's stress must accompany efforts to help parents of both genders balance work and family more easily.

A Burden of Anger

Many women carry a burden of anger, a sense of being let down and not receiving adequate support for their dilemmas. Sometimes this anger is directed at women who have made different choices, an understandable but unfortunate response that prevents women from supporting each other. Other women, if they perceive that they are carrying a disproportionate amount of the mental, emotional, and physical load at home, feel continual rage at their partners or at men in general. Hochschild described in great and sensitive detail the various paths this resentment can take, as well as the toll the conflict can take on men in these relationships.[4]

The Difficulty in Relinquishing Control

Home and children are areas where women usually feel competent and experience some sense of power and control. Some women consciously or unconsciously try to retain control over home and family, even if they simultaneously find the weight of their responsibilities burdensome. Whether from the pain of struggling with their partners, their horror at compromising their standards, or their reluctance to give up a rare and fragile sense of authority and worthiness, many women are unwilling or unable to explore their full range of options when it means compromising at home. Many women cannot create balance in their lives until they first struggle with this dimension of themselves.

A Lack of Role Models

Many women are pioneers, trying to forge new roles without benefit of role models. They lack role models of mothers working outside the home, and even fewer have models for how to combine roles in a balanced way. For many, this lack is very painful. Isabel expresses pain that her life is so different from that of her mother, her primary role model: "I think for my generation and in my community, many of the moms were home. My mom was home all of our lives. She cooked good meals, and I remember we didn't have much money, but we had the best food there ever could be— Mexican food, fresh tortillas every day, nothing bought, everything from scratch. It was great. She was there, all the time, silently."

Julie describes her frustration of being a trailblazer: "I was the first to arrange a reduced time schedule. I would have benefited if someone had walked the trail before, if I didn't have to stand alone to present my case that this was do-able. There are very few top executives of companies who are female, have children, and are working reduced time. Our company, and my industry, didn't have any role models to go by, and they still don't. Role models would have been very helpful."

Many of the women we interviewed who felt least guilty about working either had mothers who worked full time or who, according to their daughters' perception, felt trapped and limited in their roles as full-time homemakers. Sharon makes this connection explicit:

I think one of the strengths I've always had is that I came from a family where my mother worked. I remember in the early seventies when my daughter was born, there was all of that controversy about women's rights and the women's movement and whether to stay home or have a career. People were talking about how much guilt they had about working, and I kept checking myself for the guilt. It finally occurred to me that my situation was like that of many of my friends and my mother and her generation. For me, it was not an unusual role, not a different role. A support for me has been the role models I've had, in my own family, and as a black woman. That tradition has always been there; the women have always worked. So it was not such a disjointed idea. That's what I always thought I would be doing.

Some women who were raised by superwomen who combined work and family roles with limited support were determined to live more balanced lives themselves. "My mother did everything," says Alice. "She worked full time, raised three children four and a half years apart, drove us to all our activities, and cracked our soft-boiled egg shells for us because her fingers were impervious to heat. I don't know how she did it. I can't."

Fewer women who stayed home to care for their children cited role models as contributing positively or negatively to their decision, though some said they wanted to give their children experiences similar to those they'd valued as children.

Gender-Specific Challenges for Men

Pressures to Conform to Male Role Requirements

Deviance from the traditional gender role is much less tolerated in men than it is in women, making it hard for most men to imagine or act on their full range of possibilities. Women may agonize over issues of work and family, but many men do not even perceive that they have a choice.

Giving up the traditional male gender role is often viewed as stepping down in terms of prestige, power, economics, and freedom. Although men may gain a great deal in the process, their losses are usually apparent and tangible. (These potential losses also apply to women who have experienced the relative freedom, power, and economic clout accompanying economic self-sufficiency.)

"When I announced to my colleagues that I was going to quit my job, move across the country, and care for my daughters, there was a split," says Bill, who works as a part-time salesperson, much of it from his home, while his wife works full time. He is the primary caretaker of their children, ages 4, 12, and 17. "Half were supportive; half didn't want to deal with it and withdrew. I think it made them aware of their own dilemmas. It was the idea that I didn't have another job to go to, that I could spend four months en route to California, that I wasn't moving toward a full-time track. Most of them couldn't even conceive of doing that because they lacked the finances. They couldn't imagine the idea that you wouldn't work every day."

Lack of Social Support

Men who violate their gender role by assuming primary or equal care of home and children are prone to isolation, although many of them say that they don't care. Being so much in the minority, these men are isolated as both males and parents. "At first, I didn't know any other fathers who really knew what it was like to take care of a baby for four hours," recalls Tom. "I still find that other fathers just don't have the same relationship that I do—at least none of my friends at work. The hardest thing for me is that I feel alone. I don't know that many other men are doing what I'm doing. It's hard to share my excitement."

Another father, Julio, cares for his 3-year-old son while his wife, Rose, works for the navy full time. "It would have been easier if we had had relatives around," he says of the early days of being an at-home father. "I've tried to make friends with people with children, but I never have time."

On the other hand, lack of social support appears to be less of a concern to fathers who are trying to balance home and work compared to mothers. A number of the men we interviewed who provided primary care for their children don't see social support as very important to them. Ray, an artist and sole caretaker of his 3-year-old son, married to Lisa, observes, "Getting support from other fathers is not a big deal for me because, like I said, in our situation I know I'm the one who's going to take care of him. I don't have any hang-ups where a man stays home and takes care of a baby."

Several of the men spoke of their need to remain unaffected by others' values or perceptions. Bill gets "a kind of perverse pleasure in being one of the few men dropping off my daughters at school. I don't feel the need for support from other men who are making family a priority. The internal benefits I get are plenty." Matt, a single father who cares for his two children, ages 8 and 11, half of the time and who works in computer sales full time for a large corporation, says, "Being a little more inwardly motivated rather than outwardly motivated about what other people's perceptions are is pretty important to me."

It appears that violating the "rules" of their gender role is such a major step for men that either those who do it don't care much about what other people think and are extremely self-reliant, or they become so as a result of the experience. Gary says about his choice to care for his sons every afternoon, "Many people don't understand, although they see me as a great dad. I'm sorry if they don't understand. But I have to make it work for me."

Lack of Role Models

Both men and women are pioneers in devising new forms of balancing work and family, but men tend to have even fewer role models. Julio views his relationship with his son as very different from the one he grew up with: "The one thing I want to give Antonio—I want him never to feel like I should have had more time, held him more. I missed all that from my dad. If only my dad had spent more time with me. It hurts. I can see myself at 75 still wanting my father's love. I know I can love Antonio. I want to give him all the love I can but at the same time let him separate."

Despite the general lack of role models for men, several men in our study reported that their fathers had spent a great deal of time with them and that this example affected their own choices. For example, Bill told us, "I spent a lot of time with my dad because he was home. We did his work together. I saw him enjoying his life, enjoying his time. It seems natural to me to want to spend time with my children." Matt observes, "My dad would find ways to take off work and come out and watch us play soccer. You don't think of that when you are growing up. Now I remember. I remember him on the sidelines. I never questioned how he did that; I just know that he found a way to do it. I valued that, and I think that as I got older, it was an important example for me."

Others perceived that their fathers were unhappy working so much and wanted to spend more time with their families or that their mothers were very unhappy with the work-family balance. Tom remembers, "My mother was a mother of the 1950s—a mom at home. In the mid-1960s she demanded more equality in her relationship with my father. She came to see herself as having rights, not just wanting help. This experience made their relationship—and the whole family's relationships—better."

Other men generally value the support they receive from their parents for both their work and family dimensions. Dave is an executive at a bank who took a year to cut back his hours to about forty per week, 60 percent time relative to his base of more than sixty-five hours each week. He wanted to give more time to himself and his family, especially his three daughters, ages 6, 11, and 13. Because of his high position in his company, this decision was considered particularly revolutionary. He says that the support and understanding he received from both his parents were instrumental in his being able to make this choice: "In my upbringing my parents were very proud of my career," he says, "but they were also supportive of the other side, of being a parent. They felt it was just as important to be involved. Other things like family values, friendships, love, and giving were all emphasized."

Pressure to Provide Economic Support

Many men continue to feel great pressure to be the primary bread-winner regardless of what else they do at home, and even if their wife is generating significant income. The fact that women continue to be paid at a substantially lower rate than men also puts pressure on men to continue to work full time.

In responding to these internal and external pressures, most of the men in our group described redefining success. Matt went through a reevaluation after he got divorced and began caring for his children half the time:

> I think men grow up without ever even thinking that there
> is an alternative about being able to check out. There is

never really a question of whether you will have some kind of job. "Successful" was meeting quotas in sales. I had this picture of this person that I was supposed to be: a parent, a husband, a professional salesperson. Maybe that is part of life experiences—to get comfortable with some of the flaws in that picture. It was for me. Now I like my job, I'm challenged by my job, and it gives me a lot of personal satisfaction, but it is a means to an end. I don't have to be an executive or a manager. I don't have any real high goals that I am dedicating sixty hours a week to. I like my job because of the balance that it gives me to do things that are as important or more important: take off and drive my children to soccer practice or see a game or to take time off when they are sick. I define success differently now.

Fred observes,

How you measure your success is really the question. Money is certainly one measure, but it leaves me a little flat. Obviously that isn't enough. I think spending time with kids and family is probably not important to all men in the same way it is to me. I actually like the unstructured time. Being completely driven at work and a success at work is not unimportant to me, but it doesn't carry enough weight that I would want to forego that. Underneath it all, I like simple things that were pleasurable to me in childhood and that I want to experience with my kids.

Expectations of Incompetence

For a number of the people we interviewed, success in balancing work and family was related to assuming, or learning, that fathers could be highly skilled at taking responsibility for the care of home and children. For some people, this confidence came naturally. Tom and Polly shared care of their infant daughter from the beginning, while both continued to work part time at demanding jobs. "I didn't assume that Tom was going to be incompetent, and some moms do assume that," Polly told us. "And making that assumption plays a role in why it doesn't work. I don't think that was ever our assumption, partially because he was always interested in children. When we would go to someone else's house, he would spend much more time playing with their children than I would." Tom adds, "But still, sometimes I haven't a clue about what our daughter needs and Polly will help, and vice versa."

Other couples experience more struggle regarding this issue. When Julio assumed primary responsibility for the care of his 6-week-old son, he recalls being "overwhelmed at the beginning with a colicky newborn. I didn't like this kid taking all my time." His wife, Rose, says she was extremely nervous at first: "I worried if everything would be all right. I was tense and didn't feel adequate at either home or at work. I used to worry about the baby—not about how he was clothed or fed but if he cried too much, and about Julio's getting mad and not being able to care for him. Still, I trusted that it would work out, although it wasn't easy. Now Antonio is older, and I feel better. I feel that home is the best place for him. I can focus my mind at work. What I worried about before, he's outgrown or we've resolved."

Motivation to Care for Children

Men who overcome all of these barriers to take primary care of their children usually value the experience highly. Matt says:

> I had pretty much made up my mind that I didn't want to be a weekend father. It was my motivation to come home to this—where they could yell at me, we could fight, where I would have to take care of them if they were sick. That gets you down to the basics, and there's no hiding. That was very important to me. If I was going to be involved with their lives, I needed to be able to see those nuances and stay in touch with them.

Marty, also a single parent who cares for his 12- and 17-year-olds halftime and who works fulltime as a teacher and a consultant, says:

> From the beginning, being a father—not just a single father—has made me a better person: more loving and communicative. Cognitively, it's made me more under-

standing about the plight of working women and mothers. It's made me a more nurturing person. I'm more understanding about the kids' feelings; I can relate to them more.

Some men say that having to fight for their right to be fathers strengthened their resolve, whether they had to struggle with the child's mother, the courts, the workplace, their own internal resistance, or all of these. Dan is a college administrator, married to Karin. He has four children, ages 11 through 24, including two from a previous marriage. "I think getting a divorce deepened my sense of fatherhood," he reflects. "I had to fight for it continually, but it's been a wonderful adventure. The price has always been worth it. I've had tremendous satisfaction. As my children go into adulthood, that they seek me out is the payoff."

Serving as Role Models for Each Other

The social climate for helping families balance work and home life should improve as more people make it a priority to search for balance and make flexible, creative, and courageous choices. This potential will be realized only if we serve as role models for each other. We must speak honestly about our experience—the journey as well as the points where we have "arrived." By speaking honestly about the complexities of our lives—the struggles, disappointments, losses and uncertainties, as well as the pleasures and successes—we encourage each other to be more wholly ourselves and to take risks.

Janice talks about the effect on her staff when she brings her infant daughter with her to work: "We have younger women in the office and a couple of men. I think that the fact that I was there with my daughter, quietly working, set a good example for what motherhood is—that it's not some trauma, not some horrible choice you have to make that's going to cut you off from everything."

Alice was teaching a psychology course at a large university when she was pregnant. She recalls:

I talked about being pregnant, about how happy I was. Some of the young women students came up to me and said that it was the first time anyone whom they considered a professional and with whom they identified ever said anything positive about being pregnant or being a parent. They said they'd been saturated with negative images, given the idea that if they were serious about careers, being a mother would be terribly difficult and certainly was not something they should give much attention to. They were so happy and amazed and kind of shocked to hear someone with a career stand up in public and talk in a positive light about becoming a parent.

We also need to work together to seek the social and institutional support we need to make these changes possible. Patricia describes her struggle to be a role model in this realm:

There have to be enough people who have experienced balancing work and family in order for the shift to take place, so we're talking generations. I look at women here at work who are coming back with their babies—two in particular, incredibly driven women, about my age when I had my first child. They came right back, though they had some conflict about it, but they waited too long to put the message out to management that they needed to renegotiate their work schedules. I don't offer them advice except once in a while to say, "How's it going?" but they rarely respond. Then periodically they'll drop by my office and say, "Well, I'm having this issue with my day care provider." So we'll talk about it. But usually in the workplace there's this taboo, especially among women in management, against admitting you could use some help or advice. I think there are hundreds more women out there who would never dream of trying to get some kind of support. I just wish there was a way to reach them.

When Dave reduced his hours, he also became a role model in his institution. "On a certain level, I set an example, though I didn't do it for that reason," he says. "I've had good feedback from the bank about this. Other people who want flexibility see what I did. They say, 'If the bank worked it out with Dave, they can do it for me.' I think organizations need to be sensitive. Although I didn't intend to, what I did made it okay to talk about family needs. It opened the door to the topic."

Standing Behind Our Bottom Line

Knowing what we want is not enough. We have to evaluate our needs, make sure they are valid and essential, and distinguish them from personal preferences. Without this effort and commitment, we'll get too easily discouraged when we meet the inevitable frustrations in trying to balance our fundamental needs with the needs of others.

Julie recalls that when managers at her workplace agreed to a reduced work schedule so she could spend more time with her two children, "They acted as if, 'Don't you feel lucky that we've given you this opportunity?' They felt that they'd bent over backward to give me this reduction in my hours," she says. "But I thought that if I hadn't been able to reduce my hours I wouldn't be at this job today. I couldn't have gone on with my life as it was and be a happy person. My need for more time with my family was so great that I would have been willing to change my life completely if that's what it would have taken to get it. I was at the point where I would have felt such tremendous remorse and regret that continuing in my position was really not tenable."

Supporting the family financially and caring for dependent family members are bottom-line necessities. Each of us also has to discover our other fundamental, undeniable needs regarding work and family. Our bottom line might be to be home with our children, to continue to work outside the home, or to do both. Our bottom line might require creating time to be alone, experiencing appreciation and respect for what we contribute to our families, sharing particular experiences with family members, accomplishing something at work, or making a contribution to our communities. The challenge is to find harmonious ways to meet these bottom-line needs and concerns in ways that work for each individual and for each family.

Notes

1. I. K. Broverman, D. M. Broverman, F. E. Clarkson, P. S. Rosenkrantz, and S. R. Vogel, "Sex Role Stereotypes and Clinical Judgments of Mental Health," *Journal of Consulting and Clinical Psychology* 34 (1970): 1–7.
2. A. Hochschild, *The Second Shift* (New York: Avon Books, 1970), p. 3.
3. F. J. Crosby, *Juggling* (New York: Free Press, 1991), pp. 20–82.
4. Hochschild, *Second Shift*, p. 7.

3

Building Block 2

Identifying and Respecting Others' Needs and Priorities

I see couples not having time for each other. The priorities get confused because it is very easy to justify that your priority is your boss or your job or the corporation, more so than your family. A lot of times you ask couples, Why are you working, if not for your family? What is this? I mean, the tail is wagging the dog.

—Charles Harris, psychologist

Once you've acknowledged that you must have more work-family balance, the next step is to create solutions that meet your needs and enhance the well-being of others. Parents who truly love their children and partners cannot be happy with solutions that violate the fundamental needs of other family members, and no solution is possible without mutual accommodation at work.

It is important to create a climate that affirms that there is enough for everyone and that everyone's needs can be met, at least over time. A sense of scarcity is the basis for a great deal of conflict. At home and at work, the goal is to create solutions where everyone feels included and accounted for. One person's "winning" at the expense of another member of the family or group is not a long-term solution. Discussions need to occur as part of a larger commitment to the well-being of all participants.

The skills required to balance our needs with those of others are the skills of relationship. We learn to create, maintain, and nurture relationships in families. In a circular fashion, the skills of relating are what we need to create strong families. They also are essential to building healthy workplaces. According to psychologist Jeree Pawl, "The workplace must make allowances for parents, offer full-time and part-time alternatives, make it possible for parents to come and go. In the long run, it will cost society hugely if work doesn't accommodate families. It will create a society where people can't be in the relationships we presumably treasure."

In this chapter we share our interviewees' insights about balancing their needs with the needs of others in their lives.

Children

The foundation of children's security is their relationship to their parents. Any solution to finding work-family balance has to support and strengthen the deep love between parent and child. Children need to know that they are their parents' highest priority, regardless of the work-family arrangement. Judith spends a great deal of time considering how her 75-percent-time job affected her children: "When I was feeling guilty and worried about something, one of my colleagues said, 'Your children know they matter.' And there is no doubt in my mind that my children know how adored they are. They don't like how busy I am; they don't like how distractible I am. They can't always get the amount of attention they want. But they know that they are my most important project."

"I believe very strongly that they felt that they were very much loved," says Catherine, a full-time investment consultant and single parent of three children, ages 8, 11, and 14. "It's not the number of hours you log or whether you actually get down on the floor and play Legos with them or whether you do finger painting together for half an hour or at all. It's how they feel about the way you feel about them. If you consider them to be a nuisance or something that's messing up your life, I think they pick up on that very quickly."

And Matt says, "Nobody is going to remember the good deal that I cut a corporation so that they saved lots of money. But my children will remember at some pivotal time the relationships they have with people. Those are a lot more enduring."

Parents who were satisfied with their work-family balance were relatively happy with their child care arrangements, which they regarded as positive environments for their children. Bob describes how he ensured his son's sense of security when he was cared for away from home: "I don't think there is any one formula that works. I think there's a variety. But the one common thing is that there is the perceived presence of a loving parent, or parents, that is guiding this, that's creating it for the child. The child must know that the environment is an expression of the parent's love."

Jean feels strongly that her son as a preschooler benefited from being in child care: "His child care provider really understood children that age. He taught my child important social skills. He taught me to be a better parent. My husband and I are loners; we weren't taught these skills. But our son was, and he's very social."

Good Relationships for Supporting Work-Family Balance

Several people told us that the most important factor in their being able to balance work and family was their positive relationships with significant people in their lives. These people gave them not only support for the work and family roles they were trying to carry out but also—and just as important—a sense of being loved and cared for.

"Well, I have to tell you that it comes down to having a strong marriage and a great husband," says Laura. "It's helped me enormously to have a partner who is an exceptional human being. He believes in me as a writer, which helps me believe in myself, even when I have no product. He wants to see my success. Also, he thinks I'm a good mother, which really pleases me. That helps enormously."

Virginia was a "working mother" throughout the 1950s. "I always worked," she says. "I did private tutoring at home with the new baby in my lap. But as the other children came—and there were three in three and a half years—I was pretty busy." She began working full time as a teacher when her children were 4, 3, and 1. "The attitudes of my husband and all the kids helped," she explains. "Maybe I couldn't go to some of their PTA meetings because I had my own meetings to go to. Everyone just accepted it."

It is far more difficult to make work-family choices without the support of significant family members. Sometimes patience is the best approach. Anita, who has three grown children, attributes much of her success in balancing work and family to "stubbornness": "When I started working, I definitely was doing something that my husband was very disapproving of. Only recently has he finally decided that he can accept it. It's taken the pressure off. And the fact that he changed his life considerably helped too, which I have pointed out on occasion."

Creating Positive Relationships at Work to Support Balance

Good relationships in the workplace are also important. Most enlightened work-family policies probably emerge because of the company's recognition of employees as their most valuable resources. In the words of one manager, "The company can't be more successful than its employees."

Janice worked hard to create a work atmosphere that enhanced positive relationships, and she reaped the benefits when she became a single mother of an infant. "One of the things that has helped me the most in becoming a mother is the fact that my staff is really supportive," she reflects. "We run our staff meetings using a support group model. People have felt very open about asking for support during the meetings, and one of the issues that comes up periodically is being a parent."

At most workplaces, the manager or supervisor is the key to arranging formal and ad hoc schedules and policies, so the relationship between employee and manager is critical. Polly tells us that her relationship with her supervisor has been a key factor: "Our professions are somewhat flexible. Most important, our individual bosses were flexible. My boss really understood and was completely supportive."

Tanya Nathan emphasizes the importance of positive, mutually supportive manager-employee relationships. "Even if people work at a company that on the surface looks family friendly and has won every award, they will be really unhappy if they have a supervisor who is unsupportive," she observes. "Or they can be at a company that isn't at all known for being family friendly, but if the person who supervises them is supportive, then it works out very well."

Judith David, director of One Small Step, a United Way–sponsored organization that promotes the development of work-family programs in San Francisco Bay Area workplaces, notes, "Usually a personal connection helps create a change. I wonder how you can avoid that because we're dealing with family issues, and everybody has a point of reference. Everyone has a family. It's those personal perspectives that intertwine with practical business concerns when decisions about workplace policies get made" (see Chapter 7).

Balancing Issues of Control

It is a paradox that we legitimately seek more power and influence in our relationships and also sometimes must let go. Learning to live with some lack of control is an important skill in creating harmonious relationships with the people in our work and family lives. Not only can we not control other people, we are often amazed when we cannot entirely control our emotional responses to others. This fact is particularly relevant to people who spend a great deal of time caring for children and to those in low-strata jobs over which they have minimal control. Women are more likely than men to find themselves in both of these low-control situations, and the research suggests, not surprisingly, that such lack of control contributes a great deal to women's stress.

Laura had worked full time in a number of satisfying and demanding careers and, when interviewed, was happily caring for her three sons while working part time from home. She observes, "There's a lot of time in a mother's life that is controlled by others' demands. It's a very serious problem that no one looks at, and it takes a huge emotional toll." Laura's primary strategy for herself was to make sure that she got regular, predictable time alone. Laura also knew that she was home with her boys because she wanted to be.

Often what helps the most for happiness and balance is to gain more control: getting a more flexible job or one that affords more choices, creating a more satisfying division of labor with a spouse, setting limits, taking the initiative to work for change. An aspect that some of our interviewees liked about working (depending on their jobs) was the sense of relative control they experienced there. Karl, a planning director for city government, shares parenting equally with his wife, Wendy. Both of them work full time, while their 2-year-old son attends a day care center located at Wendy's workplace. Karl loves caring for Sam, but he also is honest about the privilege he experiences being at work:

> I think I would have had trouble having to be with Sam all day every day—maybe because then the whole day I would have had to basically be on his schedule and do things his way. Being at work, I can take little bits of time to do what I need. If I sit down and read, or if I decide to go out and have lunch, I've got that hour free. Nobody's going to disturb me. I don't have to talk to anybody. I wouldn't be able to do that at home with Sam.

In other situations, some of our interviewees gained balance when they learned to relinquish or accept lack of control. To Marjorie, director of a nonprofit organization and mother of three grown children, relinquishing control was a key element in her lifelong quest to achieve peace with her work-family balance. As she explains, "I think successful family units need to operate with lots of communication and the ability just to give way, to give up control—to put something in the pot and feel that what is going to come out of it will be to the mutual benefit of all."

Anita recalls the days when her husband first did the food shopping:

> When you begin to move out of one role and into another, or even when you begin to share them, I think

things like who does the grocery shopping and do they come home with what you want become serious bones of contention. Ed had a whole different shopping list. I would think that we'd worked on it together, but then he'd come home with a cereal I'd never buy. I made a conscious decision at some point that I could either take over the shopping or could live with what he bought. If you hand over a task, you have to hand over all of it, not just parts of it.

Catherine has embraced the lack of control:

One consequence of working is that you give up a lot of control over your own child, and to my mind that's a tremendous plus. People feel very differently about the issues of power and control and needing to feel needed. I thought that the best thing I could do for my children was to not be needed. I want to be loved, but I want them to be able to negotiate the world on their own. I think the relinquishing of control—the physical distance that came with day care at an early age—at least in my case created in them the sense that they are kind of independent actors.

Skills of giving up control also can be useful in the workplace: delegating tasks, sharing a job, cutting back hours, or making a career change without fully being able to anticipate the consequences. Of course, it's much harder for people to embrace giving up control if they've never had much in the first place. Giving up control does not substitute for the effort to gain more control. Balancing this contradiction is part of the art of balancing work and family.

Becoming Conscious of Our Expectations

Just as knowing what we want for ourselves can be a complex process, recognizing our expectations of others also requires effort. Work-family counselor Linda Artel suggests that people who have assessed their own needs and preferences apply this process to their expectations of others. "Have your partner articulate what he thinks a mother should be," she suggests. "Look at how you are and are not like his model. Do the same with regard to him as a father. Find out your internal expectations of yourself and others at home and at work, and work these out with your spouse. Change your mind-set first; then change external reality."

Once our expectations reach the light of awareness, we can sort out the reasonable from the unreasonable, the ones likely to elicit favorable or unfavorable responses. With effort, we also can identify the source of our expectation: A real, current need? An old habit? A past association? None of this discrimination is possible when our expectations remain hidden.

Dinner at Catherine's, with three school-age children, is likely to be disorganized and chaotic, she says.

> We all sit down at the same time, but that doesn't mean that everybody stays there. People are jumping up and all the food isn't on the table and somebody has moved on to eating dessert while the rest of us are still starting. I might get in a pretty bad mood about that if my concept of dinner was that everybody sat around nicely and asked permission before they left the table. I could be sitting there not enjoying my dinner and being extremely grouchy unless I recognized that I'm confusing two variables here: the reality and the expectation. Just move them a little closer together, and if reality won't budge, then you have to do something about changing your expectations. That can be one of the world's most painful things.

For Catherine, the expectation that dinner proceed in a certain way was something she could relinquish. For someone else, this desire might reflect a bottom-line need. In either case, the person could not proceed to negotiate with the others involved until he or she understood the source and nature of the expectation.

Asking for What We Want

Even when you've identified your needs and believe them to be valid and legitimate, you still face the challenge of communicating them to others: partners, managers and bosses, child care providers, and children. Being willing to ask for what you want, or otherwise to try to create what you want, is the crucial next step. Several people we interviewed got positive results when they asserted their family and work needs clearly, either verbally or through action. For some, the resistance they expected never materialized. Others didn't even consider the possibility of resistance; they just assumed that everyone's needs could be met and acted on that assumption.

"You can really set the stage or call your own shots, figure out what you want, and then try to match it up with everybody else," says Fred:

> What I've found, and I feel like I was slow coming to all this, is that you can control your situation more than you might think and break the rules or change the rules. I remember when my children were young, and especially when there were babysitters in our home who had to leave by a certain time, there was incredible pressure to not be late for this person. I found the work world didn't collapse when I left to make that deadline. At first I thought it might. After a number of times with no major repercussions, I got the message.

Sherrie occasionally takes her son with her to work, and so far has met with no resistance. She explains, "Coleman goes with me to the hospital once or twice a week, up to about four hours at a time. He brightens everyone's day when he's there. I assume that since my job is mental health, they'll be supportive. I never asked; I just did it. I continue to work there because the people at work are comfortable with his being a part of it. I'm available enough to satisfy the people at work who need me."

Obviously these solutions won't work for all job situations. But you will never get what you need if you don't ask or take action in your own behalf. This fact may seem simple, but asking really can be powerful. According to Judith David, "One of the primary reasons that programs go into place is because employees express that they need them. So the question becomes, How do employees effectively get that message across to their employer? Employees can really be doing more to bring these issues to the surface and drive them."

Creating Win-Win Solutions

Creating solutions that work for everyone requires the person who wants changes to communicate a willingness to respond to the needs of the others involved: partners, children, bosses, coworkers, and clients. "I try to be very flexible," says Julie. "If a client is coming in, I change my schedule. I think it's a two-way street, with both the company and the individual remaining flexible. In this day of computers and telecommunications, it's much more feasible to make these arrangements."

If you've negotiated a reduced schedule and your coworker needs some information immediately, not next Tuesday when you're next in the office, flexibility and a willingness to be called at home can ensure the success of your new arrangement. If you're sensitive to the real needs of the job and the workplace, you are much more likely to receive the same kind of consideration. And if your work schedule changes, be sure to let others whose work links with yours know so doing their job doesn't become more difficult. Consideration of how changes in your work schedule may affect the ability of others to function—and keeping them informed—is very much in your own interest.

Jayne needed to change her work schedule when her second child was born:

> I asked the paper if I could go to a four-day-a-week schedule. They were very supportive. I have an arrangement with the city editor. On Mondays, when a big story on my beat is tracking, I work. Otherwise I don't. It still leaves them somewhat lost if something breaks by surprise. I don't want the editors here to be painfully aware that I'm working four days a week. It's worked out now for two and a half years. I have a computer at home, so if a story is breaking, I work on it at home, making interviews and calls and writing at home after five instead of staying late at the paper. I do that about three times a week if there's a breaking story.

Sometimes it is important to add the dimension of time to the awareness that everyone's needs can be met. If everyone is committed to everyone else's needs also being met over time, then it is easier to give one person's needs priority at any given moment. Laura describes how this approach works in her family:

> It's not about equality. It's not really treating everybody the same. It's having fundamental respect for the circumstances of that person's life. Usually what happens is that it is going to require something of the other person once your lives are all twisted up together. Some days—for example, on Saturday—something will be of prime importance to my 8-year-old. Then we say okay, this is the way we will direct our lives and time here. You're constantly making these choices, constantly reassessing circumstances to get them in some way to serve everybody's benefit.

Improving Communication

We're not born knowing how to communicate. The consequences can be extremely painful when one member of a couple is unable or unwilling to communicate directly to the other what he or she needs or when the response—from partner, employer, or someone else—is unsupportive. Many of our interviewees identified improving their communication skills as essential to their efforts to balance work and family. Several also noted that learning to communicate effectively was challenging.

Ethel Seiderman is married, the mother of two, and a grandmother. She emphasizes the important role that communication played in her own growth regarding work and family:

> This morning, I said, "Stan, I'm in a hurry. I've got to meet Deborah, and I'm running ten minutes late. Please make the bed." He said, "Sure." It has to do with how you ask for the help. You're not asking from a deprived, inept, not-able-to-keep-this-burden-together place. You're asking from the role of a friend. You don't even have to wait for the answer, it's so reasonable. So a lot of it has to do with the way we communicate ourselves. And for the most part, I think women tend more to communicate from an apology position: "Oh, I'm sorry I didn't do it all." And when you

come from that place—I hate to say it, but it's true—you're going to get kicked a little bit more. I had to methodically learn. Now it's second nature.

Marjorie, also the mother of grown children, echoes the importance, and challenge, of communication: "There is nothing that cannot really be said if it's honest," she observes. "I think where kids get messed up, and also relationships with oneself, and also marital relationships is when manipulation and hidden agendas are all over the place. I think this coming to a condition of honesty with oneself and then learning how to be able to say it are two beautiful tools that have been honed out of a lot of real agony."

The often forgotten half of communication is listening deeply to understand the other person's perspective, wishes, priorities, struggles, and discoveries. Listening precedes understanding. Without mutual understanding, there can be no mutual solutions at work or at home. Understanding the point of view of the other person helps us to be sensitive to their limits as well as to their potential.

Karin works part time as a nurse, sharing parenting of two children, ages 15 and 11, with her husband, who works full time. She says, "The concept that we base our life on is that there is a way to talk that you can say the deepest things that you need to say in ways that are not hurtful, and that there is a way to listen that really validates what the other person is saying without having to believe it or accept it. Doing that with each other, and teaching the children to do it, has allowed us to continue moving through without breaking at crisis points."

Judith David emphasizes the importance of listening at the workplace:

When you meet resistance, probe to understand the underlying values. What are the experiences behind whatever it is you're running up against? Then go from there. But that's not easy. Why is this person saying no? Is it because they just want things done the way they've always been done and that change, in and of itself, could be threatening? Is it because they somehow believe that mothers shouldn't be in the workplace? Whatever it is, their thinking about it really needs to be understood, and the dialogue itself can help advance the changes you're trying to make in your workplace.

She also notes that "communication serves different purposes. Are you sharing resources? Are you getting emotional support? Are you identifying problems or clarifying expectations? Or are you sharing information that will persuade or change attitudes? In that case, clippings from newspapers and magazines, showing what other companies have done, can be helpful."

A frequent benefit of good communication is that it helps people understand that their own experiences are not unique. Such knowledge not only makes people feel better, it also is often a prerequisite for social change. "With employers we try to get them talking to other employers," David adds. "With parents, talking with other parents about whatever the issues are—even just finding that someone else is dealing with the same thing—brings some comfort. Inevitably you get ideas of how you can go about doing things just by hearing how other people are doing it."

Speaking openly about the reality of work-family issues also helps others enlarge their perspective and make positive choices. People who are about to enter the periods of their life when work-family issues emerge benefit from practical information about what it is like to care for a newborn or an aged parent, how a colleague or neighbor negotiated a flexible work schedule, or what professions are more and less supportive to alternative work schedules.

"I think it's important to recognize that some workplaces lend themselves better than others to supporting the family," says Catherine, an investment consultant:

It's the nature of the work. It would be wise for women to bear that in mind when choosing what they're going to do. Some women thought going into law was a way to combine work and family, but the way the economics of it have worked out, it's one of the most horrendous careers a woman can pick because there's a relentless emphasis on billable hours. You can't make an agreement with your boss because it depends on your client. If the client calls up and needs something in triplicate in three hours, you can't go pick up the kid who's sick. It's you or the job. I do think there's inadequate information for young women when they're choosing careers.

Expressing Appreciation

Many of our interviewees emphasized how much they appreciated what someone else, usually their partner, contributed to their work-family arrangement. Letting people know that we appreciate their contribution is essential. While we were interviewing Lisa and Ray together, she told us, and him, "I think our success has a lot to do with Ray sacrificing his career and putting it on hold. He doesn't mind having the experience of raising his son and seeing it through. It also has a lot to do with us not taking advantage of each other or not taking each other for granted. I mean, if you could find someone like that . . . Yeah, I've got it made," she laughs.

Joe expresses his complete support for his wife in her work and parenting roles: "Julie is an absolute role model. She is in the top 1 percent of what she has achieved. She's superb. Most of the women who have made it in the corporate world did so because they had entered into a man's role and did not have children."

Karin deeply appreciates the support of her husband, which allows her to stay home as much as possible and care for her children. She also values his involvement as an active, hands-on father, and appreciates the complexity of the conflicting pressures he has faced:

> The thing for me was that whole image of having somebody at the door when you are in the cave with that little baby who has just been born. You can't go out and get food. You can't go out and hike; you can't go out and scare away the animals. You need that person at the door of the cave, and he was there. I think it is a hard time for men. Does he want to be a man at the door of the cave, or does he want to be a totally equal partner in it all? It is hard for somebody to be equally okay with either one, with earning the money and with you being half the earner. It is a lot to ask of men at this time, especially when they haven't been raised for that. For me, he was always very comfortable in both ways.

Besides valuing the people in their lives, the people we interviewed generally appreciated their lives and focused on the parts that were working. We were amazed at how many of them described themselves as lucky, regardless of how their circumstances appeared to outsiders.

Tom feels lucky because he and Polly waited many years before they had their first child, so he doesn't resent temporarily giving up some of the activities he loves, like rock climbing and travel. Karl feels lucky because he thinks Sam is an "easy" baby and because his and Wendy's extended families are nearby and involved. Marty feels lucky because he is able to work at home and be available, in various ways, for his daughters.

Julie, who has successfully worked a variety of flexible and reduced schedules since her first child was born eight years ago, adds a social perspective to her concept of luck: "I feel lucky, but I also wish we lived in a society where I didn't have to say that I'm lucky—where I could say, 'I deserve this time,' and it didn't have to be hard fought."

Letting People Parent in Their Own Way

Parents need to allow each other to nurture their children and contribute to the household in ways that express their uniqueness. They also need to give each other the time to develop new skills and competencies. A father who has never cared for an infant will develop the skills in his own way, although it may take a while. A mother who decides to work outside the home may need special encouragement and reassurance from her husband to combat the guilt that arises from violating a traditional gender role.

Diana is a psychotherapist who is married, works part time, and has two children, ages 4 and 6. "I knew I had to stop trying to control the scene with Jack and the kids," she says of her husband, who works full time from a home office. "When they were babies, I controlled the parenting. I realized I had to relinquish my ideas about the best way to parent, to give him his own space to do that. That's been really good for all of us. Jack began taking more responsibility, and he grew more confident, learning from his own mistakes—like taking care of Barbara's hair. The only way he knew how to do it was to wash her hair every day, and that was fine. She liked it. Or when I was on a trip, he took Alexandra out shopping. Buying clothes has never been his thing, but the dress he bought her is her very favorite."

How Institutions Can Support Family Connections and Commitments

People who aspire to balanced work and family lives may be willing to make sacrifices: reduce their pay, give up travel and interesting assignments, be cut off from work relationships. But they're not willing to be denied the opportunity to contribute to work at a high level. They don't want to be regarded as uncommitted to work or as second-class citizens because they also are committed to their families. To reverse this too-common trend, the values of the workplace must change.

Change can begin with the simple act of creating a work climate where people feel free to acknowledge that they have families and that they think about their families while they are at work. This change is particularly needed for men, many of whom find it difficult to admit that they want to balance their work and family because our culture still defines men's family role exclusively as breadwinner. According to Fred, "I think there are so many people who must be dealing with work and family issues. I don't know how many of them also experience the tension that I do. I don't know if I'm just a tense person. But I assume there are others out there who are feeling the same way. Probably the biggest hurdle is just making it an acceptable part of the work environment to talk about it, to disclose that this is what's going on."

The next step is to institute gender-free policies and procedures so people can honor their commitments to their families, and reinforce the idea that people can take advantage of these policies with impunity. Employers who make such a shift are likely to see an increase in the number of employees who are loyal, productive, and committed.

Wendy describes her experiences in jobs that did, and did not, recognize and respond to her needs as a parent of a 2-year-old:

My current employer very much acknowledges that employees are family people. Many of my peers and directors are themselves parents of young children, and people talk openly about family and managing their schedules. That wasn't the case where I was before. The vice president never asked if I had a family, and it wouldn't have made any difference to him if I did. I never would have dared to use family as the reason for anything—lateness, absence. But here my schedule is pushed back fifteen minutes so I can drop off my son at child care, and there are lots of opportunities for flexible schedules. There's an overall acknowledgment that people have to balance work and family. It's part of a broad understanding of exactly what diversity is: different values, schedules, family lives, time in their lives. For me the issue is a young child, but if I were caring for an aging parent, the attitude would be the same.

4

Building Block 3

Developing a Positive Relationship to Limits

I do the menu planning and shopping. I don't get high grades for cooking, but we don't starve.

—Bill, married, part-time salesperson, primary caretaker for children ages 4, 12, and 17

The third building block is acknowledging that we are human—that we have limited time, resources, and energy. We can't do it all. Above all, we can't do it all perfectly.

"Limits, it seems to me, are a hot button for people who act as though there were no limits," says Marjorie. "If you say I'm limited, that's a real downer for me. You're telling me that I am an incomplete person. Limits are what the aging scenario is all about. But limits also free us if we can let go. Am I going to knock myself over the head every time I can't remember something? Do I think less of myself? Well, I certainly do. Can I let go of that?"

Catherine feels that women are being given the message that they can do it all, "almost as though there were no cost to it. I think that's a big mistake. Not that we should hold anybody back, but they can't do it all without a certain amount of difficulty, and that's okay. They haven't failed."

Acknowledging limits, setting limits, and living within limits call on an array of skills: testing, experimenting, discriminating, grieving, working to change, accepting. People who have created good work-family balance develop a positive relationship to limits. This chapter explores some essentials about working with and within limits.

Myths and Realities

A close examination of limits reveals a variety of common myths:

> *Myth:* We should be able to rise above all limits. If we can't overcome limits, internal or external, there's something wrong with us.
>
> *Reality:* Limits are a fundamental part of human life. Limits are often a great catalyst for growth, change, or learning.

> *Myth:* Limits are bad or painful.
>
> *Reality:* We may experience limits as bad or painful, but they also can be helpful, soothing, restful, reassuring, or even life-saving. One of the best ways to develop a positive relationship with limits is consciously to set limits for ourselves.

> *Myth:* Limits basically are similar to each.
>
> *Reality:* At least five kinds of limits are relevant to people working to create a better balance between their work and family responsibilities:
> 1. Inherent, natural, and unchangeable limits
> 2. Unnatural, illusory, and changeable limits—pseudolimits
> 3. Unnatural, unreasonable, and unfair limits that we can't imagine how to change
> 4. Real limits that are changeable, though perhaps not by our efforts alone and rarely with immediate results
> 5. Helpful, protective, and reassuring limits

Natural Limits That Can't Be Changed

Many limits are natural laws that work much like the law of gravity. Gravity could be regarded as a limit (it prevents us from flying), though generally we accept it with minimal pain or resistance. Somehow many of us rebel against other equally natural limits and imagine there's a way to overcome them. But when we're seeking work-family balance, we have to accept them:

Time

There are twenty-four hours in every day.
A baby will be a baby for a very short time.
I can't do a task faster than I can do it.

Body

We can't carry three children and three bags of groceries at
  once.
Only mothers can give birth or nurse babies.
I can't do a task faster than I can do it.

Psyche

We can't give constantly; the psyche requires input and
  renewal.
People need to be held and comforted.
We learn through experience and mistakes.
Children need support from more people than just their parents.

Self/Other

I can't make my child/partner/boss/mother:
  ◻ Happy
  ◻ Secure
  ◻ Responsible
  ◻ Appreciative
I can't answer anybody else's questions or live anyone else's
  life.

Reciprocity

I can't have fully reciprocal relationships with most other
  adults while I am caring for a small, dependent child, unless
  the other adult also is caring for someone in the same way.
As the parent of a young child, I have needs at work that
  aren't shared by my colleagues in different situations.

Contradictions

I can't fulfill contradictory demands.

History

I'm living a family life that is vastly different from my own
   childhood.
Nothing in my past prepared me for these feelings.
I made a mistake. I thought I'd be ready to go back to work [*or*
   I thought I'd want to stay home].

These facts or feelings can't be changed; they just are. The
nature of feelings is to change over time, but in a given moment
they exist and affect us. Here are some positive ways to respond to
natural, unchangeable limits:

- Accept.
- Surrender.
- Identify and act on your bottom line.
- Choose.
- Laugh.
- Rest.
- Forgive.

Unnatural, Illusory, Changeable Pseudolimits

Other phenomena that we experience as limits are actually false
limits or outgrown limits that we can, and should, release. These
limits often take the form of unconscious assumptions about the
nature of ourselves or of the world, when a closer examination
indicates that the world in fact is *not* that way at all. They also
appear as efforts to meet what we believe are others' expectations
or as requirements that others meet our expectations.

Perfectionism

- I can't allow myself to have a crumb on my kitchen floor.
- I could never do less than a perfect project at work.
- I must satisfy all the people in my life.
- I'm the kind of person who could never:
   —Attend a support group.
   —Assert myself with my boss.

—Tell anyone at work that I'd rather be home with my child.
—Tell my partner [mother/friends] that I'd rather be at work.
—Admit that I can't do it all.

❏ I'm the kind of person who always has to:
—Be the breadwinner, no matter what.
—Be with my child every second.
—Have a child who is a great reader [musician/sports star].
—Do everything myself, never asking for help.

Above all, we place unrealistic demands on ourselves. We try to be the perfect parent, worker, person. A woman tries simultaneously to live up to the conflicting, socially prescribed demands of being a good woman—nurture the family, pick up the baby, stay home, cook food from scratch—and a good human adult—fulfill the self, let the baby cry it out, have an interesting and remunerative career, develop a fifty-fifty partnership with her husband, do volunteer work. A man tries to live up to the demands of old ideals—be the breadwinner, the person who can cope with any crisis without distracting feelings, the physical protector—and at the same time meet the new ideals—be an equal partner, a sensitive listener, an expresser of tender feelings, a hands-on father. And both parents try to create perfect children and perfect experiences for their children in a society that is seriously deficient in adequate supports for families and children. Something has to give. Too often it's our physical and emotional health.

When we are unsuccessful in overcoming these limits, we usually blame ourselves. If we can't live up to our view of who we are "supposed" to be or what we are "supposed" to do, we feel we've failed. Many outside pressures reinforce our tendency to be unnecessarily demanding of ourselves. Society often portrays unrealistic images of what is possible and desirable.

For the parents we interviewed, a key factor in their achieving balance and peace was giving up unrealistic expectations and, according to Laura, a "pesky kind of perfectionism." She told us, "You need to make life easy on yourself. I know what kind of person I want to be to my kids. I'm not a full-service mother. My kids put away their own laundry, and if they forget their lunches I don't deliver them to school. I'm not one of those mothers who's that wild about playing with my children on the floor. But if they want me to read the Tintin books, numbers 1 to 20, I'll read every one. You have to decide whose rules you're living by."

Virginia, who worked full time as a teacher while raising three children, now in their forties, remembers her family life in this way: "We didn't worry about things like germs. We took baths, you know. We changed clothes and put stuff in the laundry—real germy things, real yuck. We didn't bother with lightweight germs. We didn't make big deals about much of anything."

For men, giving up on perfectionism often means letting go of their expectations of themselves with regard to work. Matt says,

> After I got more involved with my children, work got easier. I didn't try to squeeze blood from a rock. I think this was true of me in my relationships, too. I had this picture of this person I was supposed to be: a parent, a husband, a professional salesperson. I had to get comfortable with some of the flaws that I had. I started being myself in my job, and people related to me a lot better when I was myself.

Overcoming our old limiting beliefs and habits is difficult and may require help and support. Start by asking these questions or taking these actions:

1. Sort out whose need is being served.
2. Notice who has expectations of us and how the expectations affect us.
3. Ask, What do I want to do? What is my priority?
4. Accept the reality that we can't always be liked or approved of.
5. Ask for help.
6. Watch children learning new things; follow their lead.
7. Grieve the loss of our idealized self; give him or her a loving burial.

Painful External Limits

Our home and work situations may demand more of us than is healthy. Being aware of these demands can help us make better

choices about how to balance work and family. Without awareness, we may feel vaguely uneasy or guilty but can't ascertain the
cause. Here are some typical situations that reflect these kinds of
hurtful limits:

"I'm an accountant, a parent, and it's tax season."
"I'm a single father, and the baby is sick. I'm exhausted."
"If I respond to a family emergency, I'll lose my job."
"I can't pick up my child late from child care, but I can't leave
     work."
"I'm a single parent with three children and two arms."
"I want to work part time, but my company doesn't offer that
     option."

Economics is a principal area of hurtful limits for many people. Without money, choices are limited. Dale reflects, "I don't
think, on the difficult side of single parenting, that economic need
can be understated. The consistent place where my life has gone
out of balance has had to do with economics and having to do
things like work two jobs and leave my children more than I
would choose to leave them."

Often in the face of these harsh realities, we have no choice but
to exceed our own healthy limits. Working parents must get up in
the middle of the night to feed their infants regardless of exhaustion, genuine needs for sleep, and the requirements of the next day.
"I have the responsibility to support the family and the responsibility to nurture the family," says Alice. "There were times when I
was so exhausted, I literally would black out. I would keep taking
care of my son, but I couldn't remember any of it. I needed sleep so
desperately, but I had to keep going. I really don't know how I did
it."

People must work the hours required by their jobs in order to
feed their families, and there's no reason to feel guilty about our
inability to bypass such limits. We have to transcend them where
possible, and make the best of them until we find a way to change
them or until we outgrow or outlive the situation.

The inflexibility that characterizes most workplaces is often
another source of painful limits. Many people have little choice
about the hours or schedules they work because their jobs are
inflexible and unresponsive to their family needs. Kristin told us,

"My fantasy was to work part time when I had kids. I was working at a bank, and the day I got engaged, my boss came in and said not 'Congratulations,' but almost quoting verbatim, 'I want you to know that we have no maternity policy, and if you ever get pregnant you cannot work part time.' I think he was joking about the maternity leave, but he wasn't joking about the part time. It was unavailable; it was full time or nothing. So I quit." People whose economic needs tie them to inflexible jobs lack even this option.

Sometimes we cannot change or eliminate the hurtful limits we face. Other limits can be changed—maybe not right away, and often not by our efforts alone. Seemingly unchangeable limits may involve a lack of information, lack of skill, or lack of support, all of which are conditions subject to change. Learning to tell the difference between limits that can, and cannot, be changed, and which ones are worth the effort to change, is an art. Often it is impossible to tell at first glance whether a seemingly inflexible limit is actually something we can affect. It is very useful to test the nature of limits by experimenting with changing them. As we become conscious of a limit's source and nature, we learn to make better choices about how to respond.

When we come up against limits that we don't like and can't change, we can try these strategies:

- Mourn, grieve.
- Conserve energy (avoid self-blame, resentment, anxiety).
- Build inner resources (appreciate, meditate, focus, laugh).
- Notice what inner qualities are being developed.
- Continue to work toward long-term change (for future generations).
- Get support wherever possible.
- Make choices and take responsibility for the consequences of our choices.
- Take a broad, sweeping view that embraces a larger context.

When we are up against more mobile limits, we might try to:

- Acknowledge the limit's existence and source.
- Pick our battles.
- Get support wherever possible.

❏ Identify and work toward our bottom line.
❏ Notice and appreciate small steps toward larger goals.
❏ Take a long-term view, if necessary.
❏ Revise plans as needed.

People who achieve a peaceful work-family balance learn to live with unwelcome, unavoidable limits as an inevitable part of life, a consequence of the world as it is. Many of them work, slowly and gradually, toward changing these conditions—for themselves if possible, and for future generations if not.

Limits That Are Helpful, Protective, and Reassuring

Most of us would welcome limits on stress, unrealistic demands, abuse, and other negative stimulation. Sometimes these limits come from the outside, as if by chance, and only then do we realize how much we were hurting before they intervened. In other cases, we can take the initiative to impose a limit on a negative situation or attitude. One approach is to seek limits on our actions, attitudes, and expectations—for example:

"I will not bring home work at night."
"I don't need to make a handmade Halloween costume [or go to this meeting/make this phone call/read this article]. If I do, then there is something else that I don't need to do. I don't need to do everything."
"I will limit myself to addressing my own issues and living my own life, and will allow others to do the same, including my partner and children."
"I will limit my efforts to be the perfect parent or have the perfect child."
"I will unplug the telephone when I start reading to my child or myself."
"I will give up or postpone some career aspirations."
"I will allow my child to experience her or his own pain and growth from limits."

Ultimately the best way we can respond to limits is by establishing priorities for where we are in our lives. To do so, we have to make choices, saying yes to some things and no to others. This need applies to large choices, such as major decisions about work and family, and small choices, such as whether to take a walk, play a game with our children, or mop the kitchen floor.

Jean describes the career change she made after she became a parent: "I spent a difficult year as a manager. Before the year was half over, I realized that this was not for me. It was the wrong kind of work—too full time. I was making more money, but it was not worth it. I had a little more respect but a lot more responsibility."

A good example of choosing limits is deciding to live close to work or child care or, ideally, to both, therefore limiting our options of where we live.

Linda, a nurse who works full time in an administrative position, is the single parent of a 17-year-old daughter. She lived in an urban neighborhood when her child was young, although she disliked many aspects of it—the crime, the grime, the congestion. But she continued to live there and appreciated its benefits. "I kept everything small," she says. "My friends were in the neighborhood; child care was in the neighborhood; my work was in the neighborhood. It was like a village in a sense. It wasn't across a bridge or across town. It was really consistent."

Karl and Wendy were fortunate enough to find child care near their workplaces, a factor that was instrumental to their being able to balance work and family. "Our timing has been very fortunate," Karl reports:

> When Sam [now age 2] was very young, he went to a child care center at the city attorney's office, which was an easy commute for me. Then when he was too old for that, he went into a new child care center downstairs from Wendy's workplace. It's been great for us. Other families I've talked to have child care outside the city; maybe it's close to their home, but they end up having to be so far away. It's not convenient, and it's terrible to be so far away from your child if something happens.

Economic Limits

A first step for people with economic options is to appreciate the gift of flexibility and choice that money provides. Money can buy household help and conveniences, the right for one or both parents to stay home all or part of the time, or the ability to purchase high-quality, family-supportive child care, which enhances a child's life and a parent's peace of mind. Conversely, people who lack options should acknowledge that fact and avoid blaming themselves for a situation beyond their control.

Although finances are vastly important, they're not always determinative for parents seeking balance. Some people with financial options suffer a great deal for lack of work-family balance; others manage to achieve a workable balance despite limited financial resources. Says Dale:

> For the first seven or eight years of my children's life, I had a lifestyle different from anyone I knew. When they were babies and toddlers, I lived on welfare and then I did things like make mail-order nature T-shirts. I never received any child support. I lived in the back of a child care center and cooked until Shannon was 5. Then I moved into a very low-rent situation. I was able to pull off the first eight or nine years of my children's lives by having this unusually low overhead. I wanted to be around my children, and if it meant living there in that structured child care situation, then that's how it was.

Many of the people we interviewed made a conscious choice to live on a reduced income in order to spend more time with their families. These were people who made enough money working reduced hours to sustain a reasonable economic life, but a number of them made real economic sacrifices in order to have more time and flexibility. All of them valued the trade-off.

"If we earned more money, we could travel more, go out to dinner more, go to the theater or opera more, but we don't really miss those things," says Leslie, who works part time. "I feel that we have a lot. Time is much more important for me. One of us can be there when Amanda gets home from school. We can take her to school. One of us is always there for her."

Rose, who works full time while her husband, Julio, cares for their toddler son, says they have priorities beyond money: "Since one of us has to work, I think one of us should stay home. We just decided that Julio would stay here because I was already working. People don't need to earn a lot of money—to have two cars and a fancy house. What you remember from childhood is time with your parents, fun."

Jeree Pawl suggests that people consider reducing their expenses before they even conceive a child:

> Families with the potential for two incomes should make every effort to live on one, so the second income is a choice. This practice allows parents to make whatever choices they need to as they go along. It gives freedom and flexibility. It would be wonderful to live on one income, saving the second in order to give oneself choices for how to organize life in the early years of having children. Of course, this choice only speaks to the upper middle class. But even they often think they don't have a choice.

There are limits to people's ability to put this advice into practice, particularly given the added expenses that come with the birth of a child. But the general principles—planning ahead, lowering expectations of necessities, trying to maximize flexibility— are sound.

We heard some surprising economic ideas from our interviewees. Several described the benefits of not owning a home (especially in metropolitan areas, where housing costs are astronomical). They found that renting gave them lower monthly housing costs, which enabled them to cut back on work hours and spend more time with their children. Tom and Polly, who both work part time and share equally in the care of their child, decided, before they had a child, not to buy a house. They initially regretted this limitation but later grew to appreciate it. "We can afford to stay home because our rent is reasonable," Tom says. "I never thought I'd say that. We almost bought a house. It would have been a much bigger stretch if we had."

Dan and Karin owned a house, but decided to sell it in order to create more time for family. "We owned that house for seven years and then decided not to own a house because it required both of us to work," Dan explains. "It was too much. It was better to sell the house, clean up our debts, pay rent, and get out of the market than to stay in the market, hold onto our house, and deal with all the stress of both working full time."

Loss and Limits

In many cases, limits are just part of a situation, the totality of which we chose. We don't reject the totality, but may experience some part of it as very unpleasant. We experience a sense of loss, which is inherently part of our choice.

Several of our interviewees said that they had to give up something they valued deeply to care for their children or other family members or to support the family. Such a loss can feel like a renunciation of self, a kind of death, but also, eventually, an act of love, a sacrifice that truly needs to be made, and it may serve as a pruning that stimulates new growth.

Marjorie faced a conflict between two deeply felt inner mandates: to care for her children and express herself as an artist:

> When I was married, in the 1950s, I didn't know what parenting was, and I didn't know what getting married was, and how much time that would take. I was determined to be a painter, so I kept on painting. But after I had my children, it did become a clear conflict—my family responsibilities and my painting. I would rush off when I finished the carpool and have a babysitter and paint. The children were beginning to muck around in the paint.
>
> I had to come to grips with the guilt of not being a very good parent and trying to take a measure of my talent. I thought about how many generations of women had done that. The minute you grew up, whatever training you had, you turned it over like the soil and gave it back to the next generation. The essential guilt came when you said, "I don't think I want to do that. I am for my own emergence as opposed to the emergence of my children," and it was a clear conflict.
>
> I proceeded. I gave up my painting, and I lost a lot because it was so tied up with my identity of myself. I had thought, "My God, if I give that up, I can scarcely live." But then I found that I didn't die, and pretty soon other things came into my life. That was coming to terms with my own growth. That was the first real decision I had ever made.

Others described their frustration with the limits that were inherent consequences of their choices. Elizabeth recalls:

> My mother created a beautiful home and she had beautiful gardens and there were always fresh flowers around the house. She was ultraorganized, with all the spices in alphabetical order. I get a profound sense of discouragement when I look at my own house and the chaos and clutter, and I just wish for myself and for my children that it were different. My son seems very disorganized to me, and sometimes I think, well, look at what he's living in: a chaotic, disorderly household. I wish that there was more time to devote to the household arts and to having a really aesthetically nice, pleasing set of surroundings for them.

In a similar vein, Laura observes, "I'm frequently uncomfortable with how complex the details of my life become, that they are sort of endless and trivial indeed. That is a frustration for a woman with a pretty active cerebral life. My idea of my life was with my nose in a book or writing, every day. I love working on a knotty problem—writing about it, tearing it apart, getting people organized on it. So there are frustrations."

These women are happy about the choices they have made. They also accept the fact that their choices involve limits, which they sometimes experience as frustrating and painful. They acknowledge their losses without losing sight of a larger picture.

Growth From Limits

A number of people we interviewed said they had grown from a limiting situation. Probably the simplest example of this growth is a new ability to set priorities, focus, and make good use of limited time. Isabel says:

> I really try to make the best of the little bits and pieces of time that I have. On weekends, because I am better off economically, we can go camping, we can go to the beach, we can do all those real excursions that I always

wanted to do with my son. Also on weekdays, I try to spend the evening with him, reading or talking. He's 9 years old, and talking to him is really important. I just stop everything and spend an hour or half-hour or even fifteen minutes, but at least it's total attention.

Catherine observed that coping with limits created resilience: "I think if things are not going smoothly or perfectly, that's okay. It's even valuable in the sense that all the people involved—the parents and the children—can learn to adapt a little bit. If we went through life with a complete, fully developed script, we might not learn to adapt."

Dan has two adult children from his first marriage who lived primarily with their mother while they were growing up but who also spent regular time with him. He also has two children in his second marriage, ages 11 and 15, who live with him and Karin, and they also cared for a foster child with serious emotional problems for two years. For most of the past twenty-three years he has had a child in the home under the age of 6. The demands of supporting these children, and of being an active, involved father, at various times required him to work long hours, commute between distant jobs, and drive for miles to pick up and deliver his oldest two children to their mother every other weekend, an exhausting routine that might have left him angry and bitter. Instead, he accepted the situation: "The identity of being a father is one of the driving forces of my adult life, even though I resisted it in the beginning. I got married when I was 23 because my ex-wife was pregnant. I was having an awfully good time before that happened, and it wasn't what I would have chosen to do. On the other hand, it caused me to take control of myself."

For Suzanna, a breakthrough occurred when she realized that what she had regarded as intolerable limits in her relationship with her husband actually were necessary to goals they both shared:

After our son was born, my husband couldn't really be available. He was traveling for his job, which he is still doing. It was a very demanding position. Later, I started my own business, and when our son was about 15 months, I began planning to really increase my business time. Scott and I had this crescendo in our relationship about his working. I was really upset, and when he came home from a business trip, I just let him have it. "You are never around, and Tim is at an age now where you two could really do things together, and blah, blah, blah. I can't live this way anymore. I don't care if we have a house or don't have a house."

This had been building for a long time. He looked at me and asked, "What do you want me to do? Do you want me to quit my job?" And it was like someone had punched me in the stomach. I got panicky and said, "No, that's not what I want." I got scared, because my business ideas required somebody having a steady income and if he didn't have one, then I wasn't going to be able to do what I wanted. I think he said that to me in a true gift way: He would have done it. I guess part of me was needing to hear that. At that point, I realized that the realities of his work life were a given and wouldn't change, and it hasn't changed since. Instead, I took responsibility for how I was feeling and stopped blaming him. I've gotten pretty resourceful.

Gary and his wife, both journalists, feared the worst when he was switched to the morning show and he had to be out of the house by 5:30 A.M. "I thought I would never be able to do it," he says. "I don't see the kids in the morning, but the benefit is that I get a long chunk of time alone with them in the afternoons. That's golden time. We go somewhere to play and come home around 5:00 P.M. I cook, and they can watch *Sesame Street*. When Jayne comes home, they've been sated with parents and aren't needy of her. She can come in and relax. It's a lot more civilized."

Laura described how her husband, in his attempts to balance work and family, benefited from his struggle with an unresponsive workplace. "Ron took off for parental leave, the first male in his law firm, and that was totally unpopular," she says. "The policy was never meant for men, and he suffered for it in his career. That turned out to be very good because it made him wise to what it was to be in the law. He saw the hypocrisy. So he structured his own employment, which has given him a lot more flexibility and let him arrange his time to meet the kids' needs."

Finally, Dale reflects on her experience being a single parent with a very low income and examined what she has learned from it.

It's an absolutely amazing creative process. You learn to wing it. You learn to make extraordinary things out of ordinary things. And hopefully these are values that have been passed on to my children about creating joy and beauty and fun where you find it in a society that is far more materially oriented. I felt like I started my life—a real sense of identity and purposefulness and clarity about why I was on this earth—when my children were born. I tend to see things with a sense of grace, in a bigger picture.

Like adults, children also grow from limits—something parents struggling with guilt should remember. Alice remembers when her son was afraid to take the city bus to school and she was unable to drive him. The situation encouraged his resourcefulness, she says: "He made deals with other parents to get a ride home in exchange for giving them parenting advice. They'd tell him the problems they were having with their child, and he would talk about what it was like from his perspective. They loved hearing about these things from a child's point of view, so they would always give him a ride home. It provided transportation for him for about a year so he didn't have to take the dreaded bus."

Making Peace With Limits

The people we interviewed who experienced a degree of work-family balance have made some peace with their own limits and those of the surrounding environment. A few parents said they felt comfortable with limits and weren't particularly ambitious about their work. Jean never wanted to work full time. "Instead," she says, "I focus on choices, how I can make choices as a working mother. I want part-time, flexible work—nothing else. Some people would find it a limitation to have to find work that fits into family life, but I consider it a triumph."

Other people struggle tremendously with the realization that they can't do everything they want to do or think they should do.

For them, external limits are essential, since they have so much trouble limiting themselves. They also frequently require support to make the transition to a life within limits.

"When I first had my daughter, I was 28 years old and full of ambition and the need to succeed in the world of work," says Patricia:

> I brought work home all the time. The minute my daughter went to sleep, I'd take out the computer. For her first year and a half, I took her to work with me or worked at home with her, and still put in a full-time week and then took on two or three consultant jobs. It was awful. But my husband helped me mature through this phase when I thought that my self-worth was totally tied to my work and succeeding and progressing in this arena. I think things changed drastically when he said, "Make your choice: either you have to change immediately, or this isn't going to work. We're out of whack in terms of our goals in our relationship." The first thing that made sense to me, and it was externally imposed, was limits. It was knowing exactly how much of my energy could go into one thing at one time; when that limit was reached, it was like a red light and time to stop. You need to set the limit for yourself, but you also need conditions in the external environment that say it's okay to stop.

Internal vs. External Limits

A number of external, structural innovations help people immeasurably in balancing work and family: flexible work schedules, the availability of part-time work that is taken seriously and is respected by employers, the option of working at home or bringing a child to work. However, these options won't help much unless people also adjust their attitudes about work and unless employers adjust their expectations about what people can produce. A part-time schedule doesn't help if it contains a full-time equivalent workload or penalties such as loss of health benefits or loss of advancement opportunities.

Flexibility itself can create problems. It can be a curse if we don't limit our work output. Working at home is no improvement if we use the situation to work all through the night, without taking breaks. Working for oneself isn't a benefit if we are our own most severe taskmaster. Flexibility leads to balance only if balance is our goal.

Some parents describe stress from too many changes, from too much flexibility. Diana worked part time and shared parenting responsibilities with her husband, who worked full time at home. She had organized her life to be flexible, to accommodate change, to respond to her daughters' evolving needs, but she found the net result exhausting. "The constant in my life is change," she says. "Each summer and each fall, we have to renegotiate schedules. I'm always trying to juggle my schedule—now so I can be home in the evenings more. Now I'm talking to babysitters for the summer. There's always that sense of impending change: shift for the summer, shift for the fall."

Many work-family advocates urge employers to define work in terms of output and accomplishments rather than the number of hours spent in a specific place. By emphasizing the task, the employee can be more flexible about where and when the task is accomplished, making it easier to balance work and family responsibilities. This approach works only within the context of accepting limits. A job based on task rather than time can provide more time for family or more time for work, with or without balance or satisfaction, depending on the nature and scope of the task. In most fields, the number of tasks to be accomplished is theoretically infinite. Unless the responsibilities defined by the employer or employee are reasonable and limited, a task-based approach to work runs the risk of losing the structure and limit previously provided by the eight-hour day and forty-hour workweek. People who leave structured work situations to run their own businesses or to work as consultants run the risk of a limitless, output-based existence that can be worse than what they left.

Lena, a married mother of a 3-year-old who left her job working for a charitable organization to become a consultant from her home, discovered this phenomenon: "Since I quit my job and started consulting, I have been struggling with keeping it part time and not letting it overwhelm me. Consulting could easily become full time and more. In fact, I think consultants probably put in more hours than people who have nine-to-five jobs."

The Bottom Line: Limits Imposed by the Needs of Children

People who achieve a positive work-family balance give high priority to the well-being of their children and to the value of preserving their own peace of mind. Workplaces that help their employees balance work and family also give high priority to the needs of their employees and acknowledge that employees are people with limits. The fact that children require care during their vulnerable years imposes a real limit on parents and, realistically, on society. Children are not productive and cannot reciprocate immediately for the care that they receive. Children and other dependents such as elderly parents are a biologically determined bottom line.

"When women care for children, it's considered natural instinct," comments Laura. "In actuality it's the ultimate, core responsibility: to allot to the child what the child needs. Anything else is secondary."

5

Building Block 4

Embracing Change and Developing a Positive Relationship to Time

It's always a changing balance. Marital status, your child's age, your financial situation—everything will change. None of it is set. I recommend the relentless pursuit of flexibility to accommodate your family.

—Jean, married, part-time career counselor, one child, age 9

One striking quality of the people we interviewed who were happy with their work-family balance was their ability to embrace change. They tended to see themselves and their children as developing, to view the happy and painful times in their lives as temporary. They were inclined to have a broad perspective of time and to view their present situation as a brief moment in a much larger picture. Catherine exemplified this positive approach. "I think I'm lucky in that I had to deal with change a lot when I was growing up," she says. "So doing something radically different may be difficult, but it's also tremendously exciting."

Gary experienced more difficulty with change yet approached it constructively. "I'm forever dealing with change," he explains. "I'm always trying to keep it stable, but other things keep coming into play. The boys have new needs, desires. Now they want to have sleep-overs. There's a soccer team. Jayne is talking about applying for a fellowship, to do something different for a while. What would that mean? I'd like not to resist change, but I have just about everything I want in this life. I like my life. I want to keep on liking it. Still, I know things will change."

Patricia observes, "I don't think there is ever a singular point of balance. As you mature as a working woman with kids, you change, your life changes, so balance becomes something different."

Diana could barely recall the "early years" with her children, even though they were only 6 and 4 years old at the time of the interview: "It's hard to remember because it changes constantly. There is constant reorganization, depending on people's changing needs."

Expectations

We asked interviewees how the reality of combining work and family differed from their expectations. With remarkable frequency, they said they expected only that they'd be surprised, and they always were.

Tom planned to take off two weeks after his wife, Polly, gave birth, but he left up in the air how much he'd work when he returned. "I had no concept of how interested I would be in staying home with the baby," he says. "I just looked at it as a total unknown."

Polly recalls, "We'd planned that I would go back to work half-time between three and six months after the baby came, and Tom would be home half-time from three to six months, but we were sort of fuzzy as to what was going to happen after that. We also didn't know what was going to happen with Tom between two weeks and three months, when I was still home all the time—whether he was going to go back to work full time or cut back or what the story was going to be." At the time of the interview, both had been sharing their daughter's care and working part-time for two years.

Ray says that when his son was born, he had no idea he would be staying home to care for him:

> When he was born, Lisa did everything. I didn't feed him,
> I didn't change his diapers. I just carried him during those

first six weeks. Then Lisa's employer needed her to go back to work earlier than we had expected, and I said I'd take care of Zachary. I figured out how to use the diapers. He was a really easy baby. I was able to do my work by just putting him in my backpack. It went on for six months. And then it went on for a year. It kept going.

Ray still cares for their 3-year-old full time.

Julio, who also cares for his son full time while his wife works, had a similar spontaneous approach: "The way things have worked out for us is we don't plan too much. We just do. We come across what works."

Others indicated that they anticipated change. They focused on transient phases of their life, specific periods in their child's development. They didn't expect themselves or those around them to remain consistent.

"When our first child was born, I really wanted to show that in all ways my life could go on just as it had without a child," says Elizabeth.

It was a point in my life where settling in on a career was very important to me, and I wanted to prove to myself that I could have a career, that I could have a baby, that I could do everything I wanted to do, and that I could continue being myself. My favorite pictures of myself were nursing when I was at the computer terminal. My favorite advertisement was of a mother typing in bed with her glasses and her books and her baby.

Five years later, when my second child came along, I had a full-time job and I took a three-month leave. I consciously kept my work at arm's distance so I could enjoy being the mother of a baby and a 5-year-old and stay home and think about homely things and kind of nestle into the comfort of the house, the food, the furniture, take naps, even, amazingly, get bored, which I did a couple of times. It was such a dramatically different experience for me that I wanted to savor it and did.

The eras keep changing in what the balance is between work and family. My current balance is one where I cut back on work as much as possible and do my best to confine it to nine to five. I try not to come in week-ends or miss nights at home. I'll carry home work and read in bed but that's hardly work. I can even confuse that with pleasure.

Janice appreciated that the people around her supported the changes she was experiencing. "I think my friends and cowork-ers all expected something to change and that really helped because something did change," she says. "If they had expected me to be the same way I was before I had a baby, it would have been really difficult. I've definitely slowed down, and what that means is that I'm no longer pretending to do everything all at once."

Many people have specific expectations of how they will bal-ance work and family, and they believe that their priorities are immutable. Experience usually challenges both. The ability to adjust to a reality that differs from preconceptions characterizes people who are able to create a harmonious work-family balance. Recalls Julie:

> I was always programmed to excel at school—to excel at everything I did. I connected reducing my hours with not being at that level of excellence. I changed as a result of my experience. I had a plan, a business school type of plan, about how it would be. The moment our child was born, I realized the plan didn't fit with how I felt about the baby and how I was going to integrate the baby into our lives. The whole plan had missed how I felt about our chil-dren and the amount of time and involvement that I really wanted to commit to them.

To Every Time There Is a Purpose

Time is precious. The time that we have for our lives is limited, and the time that we have to be with our children is even more limited. An awareness of time limits can make us value our time more and use it wisely, make us crazy and grief stricken, or do both. One of the greatest challenges facing most working parents is a perceived lack of time, or the sense of a huge disparity between the time available and the number and variety of demands. Our interviewees dealt with limited time in a variety of ways. A positive consequence of being aware of the passage of time can be an ability to appreciate the moment.

Julio says about his relationship with his 2-year-old, "I don't live for the future, for what I'm going to give to him in the future. I give to him now. I give him time."

Closely related to the idea of appreciating each moment is the value of getting the big picture, viewing the present from the perspective of the total life span. Polly shifted her perspective about time when she contrasted the span of her work life with the span of her daughter's childhood: "If I stayed here at my job for five years, I realized what a small proportion of my working life it would be, but what a huge proportion those five years are of a child's life. I had a timetable in my mind. I shifted."

Part of the big picture is the idea that people can experience different aspects of life over time. A baby will not always be a baby. A special project will not always require extra hours at work. Focusing on the short time that children are young seems especially to motivate parents to create balance in their lives.

"Early on, when I had my first child, it struck me that nothing lasts forever. I use that as a very strong guiding principle in my own sense of patience and self-understanding. The beauty of my children is not going to last forever," says Laura of her three children, ages 2, 4, and 8. "It breaks my heart, and I can barely stand to think that thought. But it's important because it keeps me moving in my direction. It keeps me knowing and cherishing those moments that we spend together, even when they're cranky, even when their manners stink at the table."

Craig has two children, ages 2 and 4, and works full time at a university while his wife works full time from a home office. He organized his life so that he could walk with his children to their child care in the mornings, take off when necessary to accompany them to their medical appointments, and generally be actively involved in their lives. "You can't make up the time because, especially with young children, if you miss it, you missed it," he says. "When I was changing my son's diaper, sometimes the thing that got me to do it was that I'd say to myself, 'You know, you're never going to get to do this again.' "

Julie says she's not growing professionally as much as she was ten years ago: "Rather than reinvesting in my career, I'm investing in the children. I can look ahead and see that I'll probably have more time for myself and my career later. I might be interested in writing an article or doing research, but right now I feel I'm really in balance with my overall needs. When you're involved in a life-changing process like children, it's easy to extrapolate that it will last forever. It won't. There is life after children." Julie has been careful to preserve her investment in her career so that she can return to it in a more intensive way when her children are older.

Ray acknowledges that returning to the art world after several years at home with his son could prove difficult, yet he chooses to continue to care for the 3-year-old full time.

> It's hard to go from talking baby talk for three years to get-ting back to talk to adults again. I have to work my way back in to see what's really happening. I know getting back to work will be difficult because the art field is very competitive. It also means going back to school and learn-ing computers because during the time I've been taking care of Zachary, graphics has been switching to comput-ers. I also want to try and stay with Zachary as long as I can. Taking care of him is a real gratifying and learning experience. I learn not only about my child but also about myself.

It would be easier for individuals to adopt a "time for every purpose" perspective if the workplace would follow suit. Patricia points out that the lack of a developmental perspective among employers makes work life needlessly difficult by forcing people to work long hours when their children are young and then push-ing them out of the workforce when they're older: "It's really all backward," she observes. "They push us out at a time when we really have more to contribute, when we're so much better and so much smarter, more experienced, more competent, and confident. Again, it's that sort of male model of success and the value of youth over maturity. In terms of finding balance, employers need to be able to have the flexibility to see that people have different needs and different gifts at different points."

Ethel Seiderman has always worked full time and now has reached a point in her life where she has even more energy for work. She says that it is important for her to be sensitive to the needs of members of her staff who have more pressing family responsibilities: "I certainly have to maintain the balances; my daughter wants me to be an available grandmother, within reason, and I try to do that. I don't have kids at home like a lot of staff here do, and I don't have new, budding relationships in my life. So I try to differentiate. Maybe I can sustain a more intense style of work because it fits my lifestyle and it gives me some kind of satisfaction. But I'm terribly careful to make that differentiation."

Gary and several other parents we interviewed mentioned that delaying having children made the sacrifices of new parenthood more bearable. They didn't feel that they had missed any crucial experiences because they'd had plenty of freedom and flexibility to do what they wanted, as individuals and as couples. "We spent a good decade enjoying ourselves and enjoying childless living, traveling every chance we got. When we had children, we really wanted to have them," he says.

Changing With Children's Development

The work-family balance changes dramatically as children grow and develop. The period right after childbirth is intense and is almost universally acknowledged to require accommodation from employers. Although there is no agreement about how long this baby-intensive period lasts, our culture generally lacks even minimal supports for families in the early months of a baby's life. Not until 1993 did the United States establish a policy, The Family and Medical Leave Act, entitling parents to unpaid leave to care for their newborns or newly adopted children. Different parents need varying amounts of time to focus on their newborn children, but all need some time, and most need more time than they get. Many are unprepared for the intensity of their reaction to their infants and the strength of their desire to stay at home, either full time or part time. This strong desire to be close to their babies is adaptive, since the first months of life are an essential and sensitive period for meeting the needs of the newborn child.

Jeree Pawl, an expert on the needs of infants, views the early days as critical:

> It doesn't matter if it's the mother or the father as long as it is someone who is invested in nurturing an infant. Someone should be there for at least the first six months, and, better, for the first year. The parents and children can certainly create a good relationship if this parental primary care doesn't happen, but it's better if one of the parents can care for the baby, or if it can happen primarily between the two of them. The beginning is extremely important to everyone.

As children grow, new issues emerge. For Ray, the change from the baby years created new, more difficult challenges. At first he carried Zachary around in a backpack and was able to continue doing freelance art jobs at home. When Zachary became an active toddler, Ray shifted gears:

> He'd be running around, and I had to keep an eye on him. I need to concentrate on what I'm doing, and I can't keep stopping. I'd be working and I'd think, "He's too quiet." So I'd have to come out and search for him. I started working at night and sometimes went until three in the morning, but my body would be still hyper. I'd fall asleep around five o'clock, and he'd wake up five minutes later. At first it was okay to lose that much sleep, but as it went on I got more tired. Last year I started taking short-term projects rather than long-term projects.

For many parents, the challenge in creating a good work-family balance eases considerably as the children mature. "Whatever good strategies I came up with to balance work and family, there's nothing that holds a candle to the children getting older," says Judith. "They're 11 and 13 now, so they're actively involved in their own caretaking. And they're company for me—real friends and comrades—though not always willing and enthusiastic. Some of what I suffered when they were tiny isn't there. One is the anxiety of feeling so enormously responsible for other lives."

Elizabeth can feel the mornings lightening up now that her youngest is out of toddlerhood and her older child is approaching adolescence: "Instead of doing everything myself, I can just issue orders—get dressed, get in the tub, come have breakfast—instead of rounding them up and bringing them around. Josh can even make his bed. Not that they do it all the time, but they can carry their own dishes."

Jean experienced a similar sense of relief: "Now that my son is 9, he walks to school alone. He might be alone for a couple of hours after school. He could go to the neighbor's, but he chooses not to. He's older; his needs change. It's good for him to be responsible because he feels competent. It makes it easier for me."

Several parents described the shifts they had to make with children as they approached early adolescence. Certain balances they had achieved during the elementary school years began to break down, and they again felt an increased need to spend time at home.

Elizabeth observes that, as her children get older, work-family challenges get easier in some ways and harder in others.

> With my 10-year-old, I feel that his childhood is significantly over. His life is more complex now, and it's more of a challenge to play a role in his life. I can see an end in sight to my period of influence, or there are so many influences in his life that I have to clamor to make mine heard and felt. I want to be there to see his homework from night to night. I want to understand what goes on with his friends, with his sports. I want to juggle my schedule so I can be there at 3:30 or 4:00. The physical demands are fewer but the emotional and intellectual demands are more.

Alice, who works at home, says of her son, now 16 years old:

> At some point, they outgrow day care, they get bored with the after-school programs, and they need something else. Then you either have to spend more time at home, or you set up a patchwork system, but somebody's got to take them places. The thing that I hadn't anticipated is that when he was going into middle school, his emotional

needs shot way up. It was like having a baby again. What was mostly needed was just to be there: to know his friends, to keep an eye on him, for him to see me keeping an eye on him, for comforting him if he let me, for being the target for his frustration if he happened to feel like venting it, or whatever else he needed. Sometimes the only reason I needed to be there was for him to be able to tell me that he didn't want to have anything to do with me.

"I really noticed a strain between work and family when Shannon hit her early teen years," says Dale. "It went from my feeling like I didn't have to do much active parenting into her doing some developmentally appropriate playing-with-fire things that required a lot of active parenting, a lot of my needing to be there at 4:30 P.M. At that time, I was working for the junior college, away for ten hours a day and also doing contractual work on the side. It was the closest I've come in single parenting to feeling like I was going to have a nervous breakdown. I was constantly concerned about Shannon, constantly exhausted."

Others experienced relief when their children got older, especially by the time they were late teenagers. Linda injected some levity: "It's easier now that Amy is 17 and has no desire to have a mother other than for food and transportation."

Time Management and Time Unmanagement

There are two primary approaches to making the most of limited time: time management and time unmanagement, that is, being relaxed about time. We're not going to outline tips for efficiently managing time because the topic has been covered thoroughly elsewhere. Time management is, of course, an essential tool that helps people identify their priorities and work more efficiently.

Janice feels that becoming a parent improved her skills in time management:

Having the baby helps me be more organized just because I need to be more organized, and that certainly helps at work. I have fewer projects, but I spend more time on each one and I am able to weed out very quickly what is a high priority and what would be nice to do but isn't absolutely necessary. Before, I had super high expectations, and I think I drove everybody a little crazy. Now I'm able to pick out what's really important, which gives them permission to do the same.

An important tool of work-family balance is to know when to manage time, and when to unmanage time. Sometimes it helps to be organized and efficient. Other times it helps to be relaxed and not focused on any particular goal, allowing the magic of unstructured time to surprise us. Valuing time can mean purchasing services to give us more time with our families, and it also can mean devoting time to something we really love, even if it's not "efficient."

Many people who create some degree of work-family balance have learned to be relaxed about time. Just because life is short and this precious time will soon be gone, they don't try to cling to it, to make something happen every second. Several parents emphasized the importance of unstructured time with their children—the opposite, they said, of programmed "quality time," which they feel is forced or pressured.

Says Catherine, "The concept of quality time bothers me because it sounds like the jargon about optimizing—that is, the maximum output that you can get per unit of input. 'Oh, I only have ten minutes so I'm going to make them a very rich ten minutes.' In my view, that can make the kids awfully uptight. You don't always have to be doing something. Kids like to just hang out."

Gary has a similar perspective: "I think the boys are a little more patient since I changed my schedule. Having all those afternoons out on the sidewalk, they don't have the sense that they have to get whatever they want right now or that they have to give me what I want right now. Today we can go to the park. Tomorrow we can ride bikes."

Time unmanagement—or relaxing with time—doesn't eliminate the need for or the value of time management. Instead, it's used to help us develop a more enjoyable relationship to time. Here are some time unmanagement ideas:

▫ Spend unplanned, unorganized time with your children. Lie on the unmade bed with the unfolded laundry. Throw the ball back and forth. Take a walk to nowhere in particular. Sing a song just because you feel like it.

▫ Bring nothing with you for short waiting periods. Celebrate the opportunity to do absolutely nothing, or at least nothing planned or task oriented.

▫ Do nothing for some period every day. Notice the breeze on your skin, the rain in your face, the sun on your arms. Hear the sounds around you. Notice the trees and the sky.

▫ Turn off the telephone and the answering machine sometimes. Tell everyone that there will be lots of time in the next eighteen years when you are not available.

▫ Think about what you really want to do or experience in your life. Consider changing your life radically in order to live that way. Make sure you actually live that way part of every day.

▫ Don't combine tasks. Do one thing at a time. Enjoy the suds when doing dishes. Enjoy the smell of the fresh laundry. Feel the texture of the lettuce as you prepare the salad.

▫ If you want to combine tasks, make the combination fun. Meet friends, children, or business associates for walks. Combine socializing and sharing a meal. Cook together as a family. Meet with other employee parents at lunch for an informal parent support group.

▫ Allow extra time when going to an appointment. Sometimes take a route that is slower but more interesting. Notice your surroundings. Arrive early and sit and breathe for a while in an unfamiliar environment. Do nothing while waiting.

▫ When the printer is printing your computer work, reward yourself by doing something (or nothing) for yourself. Stretch. Look out the window. Sing a song to yourself. Breathe. After all, in the old days you would be typing. If the printer is doing this work for you, the least you can do is something wonderful for yourself to celebrate this technological miracle. (Needless to say, different workplaces are more conducive than others to this approach.)

▫ Appreciate delays. Take time to relax and enjoy doing nothing if you're stuck in a traffic jam.

❑ Engage in slow activities: fishing, baseball, sewing, walking, yoga, writing with a pen, gardening, meditation, or slow dancing. Go for a walk with a toddler at her pace. Stop and look at everything she picks up. Listen to the sounds she hears. If you feel uncomfortable moving more slowly, don't start rushing again immediately. Give yourself time to get used to this new pace.

❑ Say no to demands on your time that you can't meet or don't want to meet. Accept the fact that time is limited, and make good, hard choices at home and at work that support your real priorities.

❑ Redefine your image of success. Ask, "What's right for me?" not, "What's required of me to be successful?" Be willing to accept the consequences for slowing down in a world that values and pays for speed and workaholism.

Time and Money

Many people decide to live with less money in order to create more family time. This decision may mean working fewer hours, giving up luxuries, or spending more money purchasing services such as housecleaning.

Marty made the decision to trade his potential high income for the flexibility provided by teaching and consulting. "Different people have different life goals," he says. "I don't make a lot of money. I have a 1980 car with its second engine. I don't have a lot of material things. But I have a very rich life because of the time with my kids. For both daughters, all through school, when they had the Halloween parade, I was there. I got them ready and took their pictures. I may not have been as successful professionally, but I've been there with them. I don't have to look back and wonder what happened, where it went."

Sometimes decisions about whether to "purchase" time reflect a choice between time management and time unmanagement. Gary did both. He and his wife have simplified a lot of the routine tasks of daily life to give themselves more time with their sons, ages 2 and 4, and also decided to pay for some tasks that free up time. "We have much simpler meals now, especially if we're both coming home late. Conversely, now we can make more interesting things. On rainy days I'll bake cookies with the boys. We can spend two to two and a half hours baking cookies. I used to work on the car myself, and I could still do it. I love to work with my hands, but it's a question of hours. The longer I'm a parent, the more often I take the hours. I want them for myself and for them. I'm willing to pay the money."

Joe also affirmed both principles. He says that he and his wife, Julie, "work smart" in order to use time the way they want and spend maximum time with their children. "Don't do with the right hand what can be done with the left hand," Joe advises. "Delegate it out, get rid of it, pay for it if possible. Do functions in parallel if they lend themselves to that. If the car's parked by the garbage can, take the garbage when you go to the car. Don't go to the market every day; get a freezer. If you don't want to do dishes every day, get paper plates. Don't take yourself so seriously. It doesn't matter. Sometimes just stop and do nothing. Learn to laugh and cry sometimes."

The decision to spend money to buy time may create conflicts between a person's real needs and his or her ideals or self-image. People may find it hard to hire someone to do a job they can do perfectly well themselves but haven't the time for.

"We have somebody come in to clean," says Craig. "My initial reaction was, 'A housekeeper? That's so extravagant! How could we want that? We're not really doing that? What do we need someone to clean our house for? If I just did more and you just did more, we could clean it ourselves. How dare we have a housekeeper? Are we exploiting someone?' We wrestled with those questions, and then, ultimately said, 'Yeah, we're going to go for it,' knowing it's one less argument that we'll have in our week, one less battle. We think the trade-off will be worth it."

Commitment to the Work of Change

Change often involves effort: to initiate the change, to persuade others to embrace it, and then to carry it out. Those who advocate for change must be willing to do their share of the work of implementing it. It is also important that those who are responsible for implementing change not expect the initiator to do all the work as a way of avoiding the whole process. The work of change must be cooperative.

Tanya Nathan advises employees to demonstrate their willingness to "take responsibility and find their own solutions, so that it feels like a negotiation, people meeting halfway, not just demands for a benefit." She suggests that employees start something themselves, such as organizing a parents' group in the workplace or collecting information about the child care resource and referral agencies in the area. (See Chapter 7 for suggestions about negotiating changes at work.)

The commitment to change also expresses itself at home. Parents who become comfortable with change help teach their children to cope effectively with it. Such parents create and embrace lives in which children are exposed to change and its possibilities.

"To the extent that I try to teach my children philosophy at all, I have taught them about change, because children are almost naturally averse to change," says Catherine of her three children. "Our move here from the East Coast three years ago could have been a traumatic event for them. I'm not claiming complete responsibility, but I talked about it as though it were a great adventure. It wouldn't be all positive: There would be negative things about it—but it would be kind of interesting to figure out how to deal with those negative things. Because basically that is what life is all about."

Anita notes that her three children watched their parents go through many transitions, "so they're aware that you don't have to stick all of your life with one kind of job or one career orientation. They know that change can be a very good thing, not necessarily a threatening thing. And they've seen some changes that were very threatening turn into opportunities."

Creating Gradual Change

Several people emphasized the importance of allowing change to be gradual, to occur in small steps or stages. Leslie, married and mother of a 12-year-old daughter, feels that the fact that her entry into the workplace was gradual was critical to her ability to create balance. "I did some volunteer work for the local parent information line for four years," she remembers. "With that experience, I learned about parenting and about children. Then I did one mothers' group, then two, then three. The groups were enough to keep me mentally alive, and they related to what was going on in my own life. It's just in the last four years that I've worked twenty hours a week."

Developing a Positive Perspective on Social Change

Several parents connected their individual or family changes to those occurring in a larger social context, which they embraced with excitement. Being aware that we are part of social change gives a greater meaning to our efforts and struggles.

Byron Siegel is a work-family advocate for the University of California, San Francisco, who used to work in the university's child care center. He comments,

> I'm lucky in the sense that my work sets me up for dealing with change. When you work with young children, you've got to go with the flow, and I'm applying those skills to my work now. My job is helping people and institutions change and supporting them in the process. What's interesting is that when you're dealing with change, people hunker down and they get very myopic, which leaves this huge void. So it's good to be someone out there whistling in the wind saying, "We can do this; we are going through change; here's the vision for the future; and I'm excited about that vision." The more I get on the change bandwagon, the easier it is because there's no end to my job. I'm never going to finish it. It keeps changing and opening up.

6

Taking Care of Yourself

by Deborah Lee and Chris Essex

Give yourself a distraction that makes you feel good, even if it's going to the mall and buying yourself a tube of lipstick. If that's what you want to do, it's very important.

—Ethel Seiderman, Director, Parent Services Project, Inc.

To create a good balance within a family or at work, you must develop the ability to take care of your own needs. Often when parents express frustration about their relationships with their children or with each other, an underlying issue is a need for self-nurturing. Think of self-nurturing as any activity, behavior, or thought that replenishes or maintains your physical or psychological energy.

Dale, an artist, was challenged to maintain her creativity when she became a single parent when her children were 9 months and 2 years old. "I had to keep a very important, creative part of my life alive," she says. "That has been essential to my well-being as a parent and as a human being." Dale did art projects with her children, joined with others in her community to create innovative rituals at holidays, worked as a cook at a music camp so that she and her children could be surrounded by music, and eventually went back to school to become a landscape gardener.

Linda's priority for herself was aikido, a martial art. "I am very proud of myself for doing aikido when Amy was little," she says, "because that was really a strong commitment for me to say that I needed that for myself." Maintaining her aikido practice was challenging for Linda, a single parent, because she worked long hours as a health care administrator and had to hire babysitters in order to go to classes. Now that her daughter is 17 and beginning college, Linda continues to develop her skills. Her daughter is also studying aikido.

Sometimes people focus on concrete things as embodying essential elements of themselves. Gary, married and father of two young sons, says, "You have to keep what's special to you. I kept my convertible."

Caring for Children and Caring for Self

When people become parents, there is a normal tendency for children's needs to rise to the top of the list and the parents' needs to drop to the bottom. The more pressures you experience, the further down the list your own needs fall. Yet, parents have to understand that taking care of themselves and their relationships is an essential part of how they care for their children. Those who don't attend to their own needs have little or nothing to give.

"I think that being a mother has been my most educational experience," says Alice. "Becoming a single parent is like getting a Ph.D. in learning to identify and act on your own needs and priorities; you either take care of yourself or you basically die. It's a very stark situation."

So many areas of life need more of your time when you become a parent that carving out time for self can be difficult. Working parents often want and need to spend more time with their children, their partners, their job, their friends, or members of their extended families, as well as time alone. Too much really is too much; it's not your imagination. But declining to take care of yourself simply doesn't work.

The apples-in-a-basket exercise illustrates how energy comes into and out of your life. Imagine that you have a large, abundant basket of apples, which represents your energy. Identify the people and tasks in your life that require outflows of energy. Children, partners, coworkers, relatives, supervisors, and community may require the expenditure of one or more apples from your basket, even if these same relationships, and situations, also provide energy at different times. The flow out is often significant.

Once energy outflows are identified, the next step is deciding how to maintain or replace the apples. A good night's sleep, a meaningful conversation, a recreational excursion, exercise, a cup of tea alone in a quiet house, a ball game with friends, saying yes or no to a social invitation, quality time with your partner or children, appreciation from a boss or colleague, time in nature: These are possible energy sources. Observe the flow in and out. Is your basket full, half full, or empty? Pay close attention to how apples come in and go out, and check in with yourself frequently to determine how you're feeling. How full or empty is your basket at any given time? The sooner you recognize that your needs are going unmet, the easier it will be to make a modification. If your energy already is seriously depleted, addressing your needs may be more difficult.

"I would wait until I was overloaded in those early months after my children were born, and I would say even in the first two years," Diana remembers. "I wasn't good at seeing that already I was trying to be too much or that I needed to stop sooner. I didn't ask for help or sharing early enough. That's something I really needed to learn."

Another way to understand the concept of self-nurturing is to think of it as how you act as a parent toward yourself. Let's say you've identified a personal concern you've had a difficult time addressing, such as a lack of time for yourself. Pretend that it's your child, not you, who needs help with the problem. You advise her in a way that is supportive, that gives her permission to protect her energy and sacrifice neither her responsibility to herself nor her responsibility to others. When you examine the relative ease and clarity with which you are able to assist her in contrast to the way you handle the issue yourself, you may discover a double standard.

Several exercises can help parents examine their ability to take care of themselves. The first, the Self-Nurturing Evaluation (see Figure 6-1), asks you to rate each of a number of self-nurturing skills and to discover in which areas you are and are not taking care of yourself. Take this test, and notice if there are any surprises. Based on your answers, which area needs the most attention?

The goal of the next exercise, Need Identification/Negotiation (see Figure 6-2), is to begin to focus on your unmet needs. The exercise asks you to identify one important need of yours that is

Figure 6-1. Self-Nurturing Evaluation

Rate your ability and comfort with each of the following self-nurturing skills by circling the appropriate number:

	1	2	3	4	5
	I have difficulty taking care of myself in this way		*Fair*		*I care for myself well in this way*
1. Eating healthy diet	1	2	3	4	5
2. Exercise	1	2	3	4	5
3. Sleep	1	2	3	4	5
4. Time alone	1	2	3	4	5
5. Time with partner	1	2	3	4	5
6. Time with family	1	2	3	4	5
7. Play time (recreation, hobbies, sports)	1	2	3	4	5
8. Spirituality	1	2	3	4	5
9. Setting realistic expectations	1	2	3	4	5
10. Setting limits	1	2	3	4	5
11. Self-comforting	1	2	3	4	5
12. Personal growth/ development	1	2	3	4	5

Source: The Center for Work and the Family, copyright © 1994.

Figure 6-2. Need Identification/Negotiation

Identify an important need of yours which is currently unmet or
insufficiently met:

Think of a specific change you might wish to negotiate with your
partner, self, and/or supervisor/employer which would address this
need:

Source: The Center for Work and the Family, copyright © 1993.

currently not met or insufficiently met. Once you identify a need, the next step is to think of a specific change you can make that would help meet the need and to negotiate this change with yourself, your partner, or your employer. As you integrate a way to address the first issue, you can gradually move to other unmet needs. Begin small, and build on your successes.

Role Models: Yours and Your Children's

It's harder for most people to take care of themselves if they did not grow up with parents who provided good role models. People whose parents neglected them or neglected themselves often find it hard to strike a good balance in caring for themselves and their own children. Sometimes just recognizing a connection to patterns learned in the family of origin is enough for parents to make changes toward healthier balance.

Parents who have difficulty taking care of themselves need to realize that they are now the role models for their children. By their actions and counsel, they teach their children to care for themselves and for others and let them know that they are capable and worthy of self-care. Some parents are inspired by their positive and negative role models: They want to pass on to their children good things that they experienced or want to give to their children what they longed for and didn't experience. Others may need counseling to make the changes they desire. It is extremely satisfying and empowering for parents to recognize that they can break unhealthy patterns passed down from their family of origin. As one mother put it, "The buck stops here."

Time for Yourself

Many interviewees said finding or creating time for themselves wasn't easy, but they regarded it as essential. Just to read this (or any other) book, to do any of the exercises in this chapter and later chapters, or to think about your needs, let alone to address them, requires time alone and time with other adults. Different people need different amounts of time to themselves, but most parents of young children don't get enough.

Self-nurturing is highly personal and takes many forms. What works for one person may not work for another. Time for yourself isn't necessarily time alone; it is time that you choose and that is free of other demands. For some people it is time that is not structured, time for rediscovery of inner rhythms. For others, the time is highly structured and disciplined.

Gary says, "I live for my children, but I need discretionary time. When I'm with the kids, I want to give to them totally—anything less doesn't work—but I still want something to be left for me. I will guard my special time." Gary and Jayne staggered their work schedules so that each has a day to themselves, and each has significant time with the children. In return for leaving the house every day at 5:30 A.M., Gary has two hours free every afternoon before he picks up his sons from school.

Another parent who guards her time alone ferociously is Laura: "It's like a little deal I made with the universe. I will play the forty-second game of Candyland, but I have a few untouchable moments when absolutely, positively, I am not available to anyone on the whole damn planet except myself. Perhaps there are a lot of women who would have a difficult time with that emotionally; maybe they would feel they were doing something terrible to their children. I don't know; maybe I am. I may well be. I refuse to speculate."

In addition to the inherent value of time for themselves, several interviewees also noted that they had to have time alone to replenish their own resources to care for their children. Most parents find that the more energy they have, the healthier, more constructive they are in responding to their children.

Alice's memories of her earliest days as a single parent are vivid:

> The first three months after my son was born, I was a graduate student, working as a teaching assistant, and I took him to work with me. The rest of the time we were home together. I discovered quickly that being with him all the time wasn't going to work for me. I remember leaving him with somebody for an hour or so and going off and having a little heart-to-heart talk with myself. I explained to myself that I had two choices: get somebody to come and spend time with him one or two hours, preferably every day, or check myself into a mental institution. It didn't make any difference whether I thought this was right or wrong. Pick

one. I decided that the child needed a parent who wasn't in an institution. That was reason enough. I wasn't contemplating working; I was contemplating breathing. From that time on I found a combination of friends, neighbors, and babysitters who were willing to spend time with him so I could have a little time to myself.

Concrete Support for Taking Time for Yourself

Like most other aspects of creating balance, both a shift in attitude and external support are necessary to create time for oneself. Concrete factors make a huge difference: money to pay a babysitter or hire a housekeeper, a partner who shares the responsibilities, opportunities for part-time or flexible employment, paid vacations, trusted and involved friends or relatives. Obviously it's much easier if there are two partners actively caring for the children because they can spell each other for breaks. Even two parents are usually challenged to make sure that both have time alone, time with the children, family time, and time to be alone together.

Joe and Julie have given time for their relationship top priority. "Julie and I go out alone together once a week," Joe says. "We're number one. We put time into our relationship." Joe and Julie are able to hire someone to care for their children in their home, which helps them to take this time.

"On weekends we usually split days—you don't have to spend both days all together as a family," Gary says of his wife, Jayne, and their children. "We switch off. One takes one kid, one another. Or one of us takes the kids half the day and the other takes them the other half. The boys get better parents who really want to be with their children." At the time they were interviewed, they still were working on their schedule to create more time for the two of them to spend together as a couple.

Linda found that a gradual increase in her income made a huge difference in her ability to create balance. "I've just now gotten enough money where I can afford a housekeeper," she says, "which has done immeasurable amounts to creating some time in my life so I can do other things."

Even people who work part time are challenged to find private time. Typically parents arrange child care only for the hours they are working. Those who work full time and rush to pick up their child before the day care center closes may have no alternatives, but part-time workers or those with flexible hours can schedule child care of one kind or another for more hours than they are actually working. These kinds of solutions work only if the work and child care situations are flexible enough and if the person considers spending the time alone a high enough priority.

Making Time for Yourself a Priority

Attitude is also essential. Even in the most flexible of situations, people won't take time for themselves if they don't believe they deserve it or if they don't make it a priority. Conversely, even in the most stressful and limited circumstances, people who consider time to themselves as essential to survival will find a way to get it. When The Center for Work and the Family gives workshops on a variety of work-family topics—for example, stress management—there is always a focus on the need for self-nurturing. Without giving themselves permission to address their own needs, participants are not going to be able to manage their stress. Once there is permission, people explore creative, individualized ways to take care of themselves.

Mothers tend to feel guilty about spending more time away from their children if they already are working outside the home. This guilt may arise because working outside the home represents a departure from the traditional mother role. Some women feel particularly guilty about spending time away from their children in order to do anything pleasurable for themselves. Men seem much less conflicted about this issue, though they frequently have just as much trouble with external barriers, such as jobs with many demands and inflexible hours.

"I wasn't taking the breaks I needed," says Diana:

> For my birthday, I took a retreat for myself, a long weekend. I made a commitment that twice a year I would go away alone for a long weekend. I also decided to take some regular time alone during the week. It was hard to ask for that. At first I just took a pseudobreak: I flew home with the baby for a family obligation. But then I started taking real breaks, trusting Jack and just letting him do more. That's been really good for all of us. So now I go

away twice a year, take breaks regularly, and meet monthly with a group of women. But most of all I need quiet space. I'm with people so much of the time. It would be easier if this space weren't so important. I still think I shouldn't need it, even though it's so apparent. To be around people is not a retreat. I need to listen to that and honor that for myself.

It often takes some experience before people realize how much they need time for themselves. Ethel Seiderman emphasizes that it took her many years to learn to take time for herself: "I am one of those people who can work a fifty- or sixty-hour week and can't reach for the balances. So I've had to teach myself to do the things that make me feel good. It is critical for me now that I get away for a three-day weekend. Now maybe everybody can't afford a three-day weekend, but what they can afford is a few hours away for themselves."

Sometimes the limitations related to finding time for ourselves are so painful that it hardly seems worth the trouble. It may seem more bothersome than helpful to take fifteen minutes when we really need at least half a day. It can be agonizing to take a little time and begin to experience our needs and feelings and then have to shut them off prematurely and return to service. Nonetheless, it is worth the trouble. Rediscovering who we are helps us to be better parents.

Creating Time for Yourself When There Isn't Any

Here are some suggestions that our interviewees said helped them create time for themselves:

- Take time for yourself before you come home from work. Walk home if you can, or park the car somewhere on the way and take a short walk. Or sit and watch the sky, the wind in the trees, or the rain. Spend a few minutes daydreaming. Even a short break can make a big difference.
- Get up early in the morning, before your children. Appreciate the opportunity to experience peace and quiet and your own rhythms for a few minutes before you begin to focus on the needs and energy of others. Sit quietly or have a cup

of tea, read the paper, listen to music, remember your dream. Do something nurturing that allows you to focus on yourself.

▫ Regularly or occasionally drop your children off earlier in the mornings so that you can spend an hour or half an hour alone before going to work. One mother took her daughter to child care early, then returned home so that she could play music while she cleaned her house. Another had a regular date with herself at a café near her son's preschool, where she spent half an hour between dropping him off and going to her office.

▫ When you come home from work, take time to collapse, alone or with others. Some people lie down with their children on the bed or on the floor. Others go for a walk with everyone in the family. It helps to have some healthy snacks so you can delay dinner. Nourish transitions; they tend to be difficult for everyone. Lower your expectations for order and structure during times of transition.

▫ Exercise. It's easier said than done, but it makes a huge, positive difference. Find some kind of exercise that you like. Find ways to combine exercise with everyday life activities. Exercise with your children or partner. Meet friends or colleagues for walks instead of meals. Conduct meetings while walking. Take the stairs instead of the elevator. Exercise is much easier if it becomes a habit or routine part of your week and a spontaneous part of life.

▫ If you are adding time for yourself, probably something else will have to go. Is there something you can give up in order to give yourself special time? What's really most important right now—not what should be the most important, but what is actually most important? Sometimes what is most important is having enough time to focus on what is most important. If you have no idea what you need, then you probably need more time for yourself.

▫ Schedule regular time for yourself daily, weekly, or monthly, in long or short increments, depending on your needs, preferences, and circumstances. Regard these appointments as top priorities. Arrange child care and privacy. Go away yourself, or make everyone else go away. If these appointments are regular, it will be easier to remember to take this time for yourself.

❑ Understand that time alone might not be pleasant at first. If you haven't had time for yourself for a long time, being alone or focusing on your own needs will feel strange. You may experience a whole well of feelings that you haven't had time for: grief, rage, despair, or disorientation, as well as excitement, pleasure, curiosity, and relaxation. New parents frequently describe a sense of paralysis when the baby finally takes a nap. What to do first: bathe, straighten the house, read one section of the paper, make a telephone call, nap, cry, eat, or go outside and just sit?

❑ Fifteen minutes (or more!) before you go to sleep, stop doing tasks and chores, and do something, or nothing, for yourself.

❑ Create a diverse, supportive, multi-age community for yourself and for your child so that you see that your child is enriched rather than deprived when he spends time away from you.

❑ Celebrate every tiny thing you accomplish, and have networks of friends and family members who know what you're talking about and celebrate with you. Honor the occasion when you put all the laundry away. If you recycled your children's outgrown clothes, rejoice. Congratulate yourself, and each other, when you've managed to add some soil to the anemic plant, complete a project at work, arrange a carpool, balance a checkbook, or take five minutes for yourself. These are no small accomplishments when you are balancing work and family.

7

Negotiating for Change at Work

by Barney Olmsted
of New Ways to Work

The most important thing to me is the feeling of flexibility with
my time.

—Sharon, single parent, full-time college professor,
one child, age 16

The prevailing theme of all our parents' stories is that after they have
gone through the building block processes, the demands of work still
challenge their ability to achieve an acceptable balance in their lives.
But the bottom line was that even though "balance" and "acceptable" had different meanings depending on whom we were talking
to, with perseverance, parents could find a tolerable formula.

The spectrum of attitudes about work ranged widely. "It is a
struggle to balance my work because I love it so much," says
Isabel. "I've never regretted that I didn't work harder on my

Established in 1972, New Ways to Work's primary focus has been to encourage experimen-
tation with work time options—job sharing, work sharing, time-income trade-offs, flextime,
flexplace, and various types of leaves—as a means of addressing employment-related social
and economic issues. These new scheduling arrangements represent strategies for balancing
work and family, spreading existing hours of employment over a wider labor force base,
improving organizational profitability, and creating ways for students, older workers, and
dislocated employees to make a successful transition from one stage of life, or one career, to
another.

career. I have sometimes regretted that I didn't let myself have the experience of only having to dance to one rhythm," says Judith. And observes Leslie, "I love my work, but it's still just a job. I don't think of myself as a career person."

These comments affirm the need for using Building Block 1 (see Chapter 2): It's very important to *identify and act on our real needs and priorities*. This is critical to our ability to function well. Employers need to understand this too. Large organizations often spend considerable sums on stress management and substance abuse programs for their employees but disregard the source of the problem. One source of stress for both men and women, according to clinical psychologist and researcher Rosalind Barnett, is "a job that places many demands on an employee but allows him or her little control over how the work gets done."[1]

Being able to make choices is at the heart of achieving balance. If you know what you need but have no control over getting it, stress and frustration are the result. Barnett cautions that companies that ignore workers' real needs "may discover that they are at a competitive disadvantage: People will find a place to work with a more reality-based view of workers." In other words, they will take control in order to gain the balance they need to function.

The other building blocks are also important tools for creating change at work. Building Block 2 (see Chapter 3) reminds us that we must *identify and respect others' needs and priorities*. This applies to the employer as well as partners and coworkers. Your supervisor, in particular, needs to know that the kind of change you are requesting will help you be a better employee and does not represent a lessening of interest in your work. Putting yourself in his or her shoes as you frame a request for change will help you elicit support.

Developing a positive relationship to limits, as recommended in Building Block 3 (see Chapter 4), has many ramifications for negotiating change at work. Setting priorities is a crucial step in deciding where balance lies. Is work a potent source of gratification, or is it just a job? How would you feel about slowing your career advancement or putting it on hold for a while? Does your partner have work options that might complement and support changes you want to make? Do you have friends whose experiences can provide you with a model or some insight about how to find balance?

"I'm not giving up career opportunities to do household chores," explains Julie, who had just cut back on her full-time job as an investment manager. "I'm clear with everyone that my time at home is to be with the children. I'm conscious about what I'm doing and why. I carefully plan my time at home and am very possessive of it." In other words, she has established her priorities.

In today's workplace, change is endemic. You might as well embrace it and make it work for you, as described in Building Block 4 (*Embracing change and developing a positive relationship to time*). Deciding how you can best use your time to achieve your work and family goals provides the basis for an action plan that will begin to turn your priorities into realities.

Creating Change: Whose Responsibility Is It?

Some people we interviewed feel that work-family balance succeeds best if individuals set priorities, make choices, and take responsibility for the consequences. Others believe business should take the initiative and change its policies and culture. In reality, both need to happen. Both sides have reasons to change as well as real (and some not-so-real) limitations that make change difficult.

Just as individuals must sort out apparent needs from real needs and identify which ones are merely preferences or old habits, the workplace too must assess its practices and demands. Some employment policies are leftovers from tradition and assembly-line practices. Often the spirit has been lost, and only the rules remain: more emphasis on hours on the job than productivity; jobs defined as nine to five when seven to four or ten to six might be more appropriate to the task and the worker; insistence on standardization when flexible work arrangements could reduce costly turnover, absenteeism, and downtime on the job. The valid limits for employers are those imposed by the cost of doing business and the requirements of providing service or producing goods. The real experience of growing numbers of employers indicates that supporting good employees in their efforts to create more balance in their lives improves a firm's ability to accomplish these business objectives.

The role of the individual in creating a more family-friendly workplace will continue to be critical for the foreseeable future. Employers need to hear from their workers that they need new options because the old ways of working are not appropriate to today's situations. Otherwise they have no reason to change. But because the need is real, employees do continue to propose new solutions.

Planning Ahead

When you begin planning how to balance your work and family life, the first step is to review your financial needs. What are your real financial constraints? Do you have to earn money right now, and if so, how much? If you'd prefer to negotiate a reduced work schedule or to stop work for a while, can these financial needs be adjusted? If a full-time salary is necessary, would a different kind of schedule help you create more balance?

There is no point in deciding that you want to stop working for the first few years you have a family or to plan to reduce your work time significantly if you have financial obligations that require a full-time salary. Worksheet 1 can help you put real numbers to these questions so you can begin working out your balancing act.

Before you start planning, you also might recall Jeree Pawl's suggestion for two-income couples who don't have children yet: Try living on one income and saving the other. When using the second income is a choice, it expands your flexibility enormously.

The parents we interviewed had a lot to say about how finances in general affected their quest for balance. Leslie says she and her husband and 12-year-old daughter can make it "by living simply. We never had a very expensive lifestyle, but we cut back somewhat when our daughter was born."

Dan has a different vision of family stability: "I took a university administrative job knowing that I was going to abandon a lifestyle that I really treasured, but I was going to make probably $10,000 more a year, and that was very important to the family's stability."

Earning money isn't the only thing work is about, of course. Most of the people we interviewed are happy in their jobs and derive important intrinsic satisfaction from work. It's hard for some parents to admit that they really like to work and need it to balance their lives. "Ben wanted us to buy a lottery ticket," Judith says of her then 9-year-old.

Worksheet 1:
Assessing the Financial Impact
of Reducing Work Time

	Current *Monthly*	*Reduced* *Monthly*
Home		
Rent or mortgage	_____	_____
Taxes	_____	_____
Insurance	_____	_____
Improvements	_____	_____
Utilities	_____	_____
Telephone	_____	_____
Furniture, appliances	_____	_____
Food		
Groceries	_____	_____
Restaurants	_____	_____
Transportation		
Public	_____	_____
Car payments	_____	_____
Car repair	_____	_____
Fuel	_____	_____
Parking	_____	_____
Insurance	_____	_____
Clothing		
Purchase	_____	_____
Cleaning/laundry	_____	_____
Medical/dental		
Insurance payments	_____	_____
Copayments	_____	_____

Prescriptions	_____	_____
Over-the-counter medicines	_____	_____
Taxes		
Federal	_____	_____
State	_____	_____
Professional associations	_____	_____
Entertainment	_____	_____
Education	_____	_____
Vacation	_____	_____
Other	_____	_____
Monthly expenses	_____	_____
Monthly income	_____	_____
Total (plus or minus)	_____	_____

A few weeks later he wanted another one, and I finally asked him what he'd use the money for if he won. He said, "Then we'd be rich enough so you could stay home." When I told him that I love my work, he looked at me with amazement: "You do?" I realized that out of guilt about being away from him, I had kept it kind of a secret that I was really quite devoted to my work.

Some parents we talked to planned for their work-family balance needs long before they had children. "I always wanted kids," says Sherrie. "My current job is part time. I took it because it offered benefits, I had the right qualifications, and I felt that it made sense in terms of kids. I took the job knowing I would soon try to get pregnant, but in fact it took me two years to get pregnant."

And Jean says, "I always had thought I would have to wait until I had a baby in my arms to ask for part-time work. A friend of mine said I shouldn't wait, so I asked. I was able to make my job part time, and I realized I was preparing to become a parent."

The best-laid plans don't always work out, of course. Reality is sometimes very different than expected, and you may have to take your plans back to the drawing board. When Lena had her child, she remembers that "at first I was mad at other women for not preparing me. There is a stark contrast between the imagining and the reality [of having a baby]."

And Craig found that motherhood was traumatic for his wife: "She had always seen herself as an executive, as a high-powered corporate person, and suddenly after our second child was born, that persona was thrown out there and she had to reevaluate who she was, what she was, and where she was going to go. At that point she decided to go into business for herself."

Workplace Flexibility

Flexibility in the workplace was the one component that our interviewees consistently identified as critical to creating balance between work and family. Flexibility generally means having more control over when work starts and ends and in some cases where the work was done.

Elena and her husband work full time and have two children, ages 9 months and 3 years. That her employer agreed to change her hours from nine to five to eight to four helped a lot.

One of the reasons Lisa stayed where she had been working is that her employer allows her very flexible time. She can leave anytime she wants for her child as long as the work is all caught up.

And Fred appreciates having a little extra time in the morning, even if he has to stay at work a little later at night: "It's the logistics—getting them to school and picking them up in the afternoon. The tension really comes up in the day-to-day grind."

Why is one workplace more flexible than another? As long as the work gets done, why should all workers' schedules be uniform? A one-word answer is "culture." The culture of the workplace dictates how much flexibility is possible regardless of policies or programs. New Ways to Work's book *Creating a Flexible Workplace* (2d edition) defines an organization's culture as "the constellation of beliefs, values, habits, and norms of behavior which actually operate inside an organization. It's the way work gets done, how people choose to relate to each other, how problems get resolved, what gets celebrated. It's not necessarily what people say/claim are the beliefs/values . . . but what actually are."[2]

Sometimes the organization culture is reinforced by the culture common to a professional area. Law and medicine are generally less flexible than insurance or banking. But even within professions, company cultures differ. Some law firms are more flexible than the norm, and some medical practices allow job sharing or flexible schedules. In your planning, consider how much flexibility you're likely to encounter in the workplace or profession you're already in or are thinking of entering.

"I've been fortunate enough to be able to find jobs that allow me to have some of that flexibility," says Sharon, a single mother and full-time college professor. "I've managed to have summers off. I did try a private practice, and I decided that wasn't something that I wanted to continue because I'd have to be available evenings and work on Saturdays."

Currently, workplace flexibility is still more in demand than available, but management culture and practice can change, particularly if it is in the employer's self-interest to do so. Employers begin to listen if enough employees say they must have more workplace flexibility or they will have to leave—or won't come to work there in the first place.

In the mid-1970s when New Ways to Work began promoting greater workplace flexibility, it was employees who put on the heat and pioneered the changes. For some, self-interest was the motive; others saw flexible work arrangements as the wave of the future and wanted to be on the cutting edge. More recently, concern about the interface between work and family responsibilities has led to increased employer interest in providing more flexibility in the workplace; employers, policymakers, and the media have all been involved in the discussion. National surveys and internal company surveys support the view that flexibility, or lack of it, is a critical element affecting bottom-line costs of turnover, absenteeism, and difficulty in recruitment. As a result, formal options that help employees balance work and personal time better are slowly becoming available.

The Flexibility Toolbox

The toolbox of flexible work arrangements available includes a number of options:

- *Flextime.* Within limits set by management, employees choose when to start and end work, and in some cases the time and length of the lunch hour and the length of the day. The program usually features core hours when everyone must be present.

- *Compressed workweek.* This schedule takes the standard forty-hour workweek and compresses it into fewer than five workdays, or an eighty-hour two-week period and compresses it into fewer than ten workdays. Variations include "4/10s" (four days working ten hours a day), "3/12s" (three twelve-hour days), and "9/80s" (a two-week pay period where employees work nine hours a day and get a three-day weekend every other week).

- *Regular part-time employment.* This voluntary, less than full-time work schedule includes job security and other privileges and benefits available to regular full-time workers.

- *Job sharing.* As a form of regular part-time employment, two part-time employees share one full-time position, with the salary and benefits prorated.

- *Voluntary reduced work time programs.* Unlike ad hoc arrangements, these programs allow employees to reduce work hours for a specified period of time with a corresponding reduction in compensation. At the end of the defined period, the employee returns to full-time status or reenrolls. This option is often used as a way of minimizing layoffs.

- *Leaves of absence.* These are authorized periods of time away from work without loss of employment rights. Paid or unpaid, leaves are usually extended for family, health care, education, or leisure time. Sabbaticals are paid periods of time off, in addition to vacation time, given on a regular cycle.

- *Working at home/telecommuting.* Employees work from an alternate site, usually from home or a satellite office closer to home. Often the employee is linked to the workplace electronically via a computer modem, voice mail, fax machine, and/or telephone.

Bringing their child to work occasionally is another arrangement that helped some of our interviewees. Janice, an administrator whose office policy sanctions parents' bringing children to work for a limited amount of time if there's an emergency, observes that "almost every week someone has a child in for a few hours and it's worked fine."

Proposing a Change

Some workplaces have formal policy and programs that incorporate one or more of these options. In others, flexibility may have to be negotiated directly with a supervisor or department head. The process in both cases is similar.

The first step is to decide what kind of change will help you function better as a working family member. Then do a little research. Find out what your organization makes available, either as a formal option or on an ad hoc basis. Human resources staff or coworkers can be helpful. It is also useful to compile information about the kinds of flexibility that similar organizations offer.

Increasingly, larger organizations are developing proposal guidelines that employees and their supervisors can use to design a work schedule that meets the needs of both parties. If your employer already offers flextime, job sharing, or other flexible work arrangements, there is probably a procedure developed. In smaller organizations the process may be less formal, but the same issues need to be dealt with. Before broaching the subject of changing your schedule with your supervisor, be able to answer these pertinent questions:

- What kind of a schedule change are you proposing?
- How will the change affect your job requirements? If your employer will have to change how tasks are allocated or accomplished, include suggestions for handling that change.
- How will the change affect your communication with coworkers, supervisor, clients, and others? What will you do to ensure good communication among all necessary parties?

❑ How flexible can you be to ensure that the new arrangement works well? Will you be available by telephone if necessary? Can you shift days or hours if there is a real need?

❑ What skills, experience, and special expertise do you bring to your work? What would the organization be losing if it chose not to accommodate you and you had to leave?

❑ Are you requesting a long-term or short-term change? Can you estimate when, or if, you might want to return to your former schedule?

❑ When and how will the arrangement be evaluated? How will any needed changes be renegotiated?

These questions will provide the basis for your writing a formal proposal. (Figure 7-1 contains a sample proposal.) Even if you're not required to write it up, it's helpful to have a "talking piece" to give to your supervisor. The proposal should contain details of the work arrangement you are requesting, the schedule you are proposing, how the tasks and responsibilities will be handled, and any impact on pay and benefits. You also should include your thoughts on how this change might benefit the organization (e.g., enhance the firm's image as a family-friendly employer, improve scheduling, retain a valued employee, save money, increase productivity) and any information on what similar companies are doing in this regard.

The proposal should be considered a first step, with the objective being discussion and eventually an agreement that benefits you, your supervisor, and your work group. If your company has had little or no experience with the kind of flexible work arrangement you are seeking, proposing a trial period to work out glitches will increase everyone's comfort level. It also gives the company the opportunity to pilot the arrangement with a view to expanding its use subsequently.

The steps outlined will not necessarily take place in the order presented. Flexibility often takes time to negotiate, and you may have to talk to a number of people at different levels in the organization: your supervisor, coworkers in other departments who have had similar schedules, a representative from human resources, your staff. This is particularly true if the culture in your organization is conservative and relatively inflexible.

(Text continues on page 117.)

Figure 7-1. Sample Part-Time Proposal

To:	John Bell, Regional Administrator
From:	Mary James
Subject:	Proposal to Restructure the Position of Operations Manager

I. Introduction

After contemplating the decision for a long time and researching options that would be mutually beneficial to the company and myself, I would like to propose restructuring my position of operations manager into a part-time arrangement. If implemented, this arrangement would save the company $5,000 to $10,000 a year. The details are outlined below.

II. Work Schedule

I propose to work approximately 60 percent of the schedule I currently work. Acknowledging that as a manager I rarely work a 40-hour week, usually putting in closer to 50 hours, I would work up to 30 hours per week on my new schedule. In selecting the days of the week to be in the office, I would take into consideration the needs of the organization for coverage on our busiest days and make certain I were here for department and organization staff meetings. My intention would be to stay as flexible as possible to the needs of the organization.

III. Tasks and Responsibilities

Along with a 40 percent reduction in my hours would go a 40 percent reduction in my tasks and responsibilities. I have analyzed my position carefully and find that approximately 60 percent of my duties are finance-related, 20 percent are personnel-related, and 20 percent are administrative. I enjoy and am best at the finance-related part of my job and would want to focus in on it. Joe Block, our department secretary, has expressed an interest in adding more tasks to his position. We could enrich his job by giving him my personnel-related duties and upgrading him to secretary–personnel assistant. The administrative duties could be performed by Grace Lee, the graduate student who interned with our firm last summer and is looking to work a few hours a day while she is in school.

IV. Salary

My annual salary after five years with the company is $50,000. On a prorated basis I would earn $30,000 per year working 60 percent

(continues)

Figure 7-1 (continued)

time. I propose that some of the $20,000 in salary you would no longer be paying be paid to Joe Block when you upgrade his position, and that Grace Lee be paid on an hourly basis for her work. I still foresee a substantial cost savings to the organization.

V. Benefits

Vacation, sick leave, and holidays would be prorated, as would benefits that are computed as a percentage of total salary (workers' compensation, pension, and tax-sheltered annuity). I propose that the company's contribution to my health and dental insurance also be prorated. This would be an additional cost savings to the firm.

VI. Advantages to the Organization

A. Retention of a trained employee. The firm has invested a good deal of time and money in training me (and others who have a need to reduce their work hours). It is very costly to hire and train an operations manager. A part-time arrangement will allow me to continue productive work during a period of my life when it would be difficult to work full time.

B. Cost savings for the company. Although none of us likes to talk about it, this is a recessionary time, and even at our company the workload is somewhat reduced. This part-time proposal will save money.

C. Reduced absenteeism and use of sick leave. I will try to arrange medical and personal appointments on my days off rather than taking time from work. Studies have shown that part-time employees miss proportionately fewer days than full-time employees.

D. Higher productivity. Studies and anecdotal reports from employees have shown that part-time employees have more energy to devote to their jobs. Instead of being time-oriented, they can be task-oriented. This translates into higher productivity.

E. Enhance the firm's image as a forward-thinking, innovative organization. Other firms that have implemented "family-friendly" work options have benefited from free, positive publicity given to them by both local and national media. This could happen to our company too.

VII. Implementation

I propose that we try this arrangement on a six-month trial basis, to begin on September 1. At the end of the trial period, we can discuss how it is working and whether it should continue. If either of us is dissatisfied, we could be free to terminate the arrangement. I would expect, however, to work hard at making the arrangement successful and to satisfy the needs of the organization.

VIII. Additional Thoughts

Between now and the year 2000, women will comprise 65 percent of new entrants into the labor force. Within our industry this percentage will be even higher. A struggle exists for today's professional working mothers who attempt to balance career goals and family commitments. Employers concerned about retaining top performers will need to be flexible to accommodate women's needs or lose some of the best women to those companies that do. Reshaping work schedules to help a woman raise a family is foreign to corporate culture. However, employers are moving to protect their investment in top performers. Part-time employment is a viable solution utilized by employers to retain quality employees.

Thank you for your time and your consideration of this proposal. I feel positive that this arrangement will work well and look forward to receiving your comments. I am, of course, available to discuss this possible work alternative with all parties interested.

Source: New Ways to Work, San Francisco, California.

"Find an owner," advises Rosemary Mans, vice president of flexibility programs at the Bank of America. An "owner" or "champion" is someone who will take responsibility for managing the process of change in your organization—someone who has taken a lead role in encouraging more flexibility or who is high enough in the company to be able to do so and is sympathetic to the issues.

Developing a special strategy or hook is another way to position your request favorably. Jayne, a journalist who works 80 percent time, says:

The ethos is that if you're dedicated, you work long hours. To maintain quality I had to have work that valued knowledge of complex issues, not valued for having my body there, long hours, or travel ability. I created a specialty for myself—health—and thought it was marketable. What changed was not my commitment to work but how I viewed work.

Your request may meet with unanimous approval, but more likely you'll run into at least some opposition because nonstandard work schedules and off-site work are still new concepts. Also, most employers still have a gender-based mind-set about family responsibilities. They may understand that women have to work a "second shift" at home, and so are more willing to accommodate female employees' needs, but they're less likely to support men's desires for more family time. Although work-family policies and programs must by law be gender neutral, men usually find it harder than women to negotiate flexibility.

The men in our interview group who were able to change or reduce their work schedules in order to take on more family responsibility are pioneers. They and others are helping to change the culture of the workplace. One father who had negotiated with great difficulty a three-quarter time schedule to complement his wife's part-time schedule gave us an update on his workplace. He reports that "at a recent meeting a big shot announced that he and his wife are adopting a baby and he is going on indefinite half-time status."

If you get opposition to your request, don't take it personally. Remember that flexible work arrangements are a relatively new idea, and they run counter to traditional ideas of how work should be organized and managed, as well as to who should do what in the family. Whether you are talking to a coworker, supervisor, or another concerned member of your workplace, keep the discussion focused on answering their concerns about the work issues. If you reassure them that you'll fulfill your commitments and responsibilities, that you'll maintain communication with coworkers and supervisors, and that you'll be flexible to make sure that things run as smoothly as before—or more so, since a source of serious stress will be removed—opposition may change to support.

Working Flexibly

Once you have arranged to work a nonstandard schedule, you may find that part of the trade-off for your new situation is being viewed differently by your coworkers, especially if you have negotiated a reduced schedule. Opportunities for career advancement may seem restricted, and coworkers or supervisors may feel you are less serious or committed than your full-time colleagues. Not so, says Lotte Bailyn of MIT's Sloan School of Management. In her book *Breaking the Mold: Women, Men and Time in the New Corporate World*, she says that:

Flexible arrangements and other organizational responses to employees' family needs do not necessarily undermine an employee's commitment to organization goals. A study by the National Council of Jewish Women, for example, has shown that when employers are accommodating and flexible in their policies, pregnant women take fewer sick days, work later in their pregnancies, are more likely to spend time doing things related to their jobs outside regular work hours without compensation, and are more likely to return to their jobs after childbirth. . . . These employees actually became more committed in response to the flexibility they were allowed.[3]

This is a lesson much of corporate America still has to learn. Many working parents who have negotiated a flexible working arrangement feel like anomalies in an organizational culture that equates long hours with productivity. This is still the price of being a pioneer in the workplace. The rewards are in the increased balance and the knowledge that you are breaking new ground for others who have the same needs.

Patricia negotiated work changes, but she acknowledged the cost:

When I accepted this job offer, I set limits in terms of the parameters of the travel. I said I can understand that travel is part of my job, but what I need to know is that I can have a balance: no weekends, nothing longer than five days on the road. Except for one back-to-back trip, I've done it for a year. I hope to maintain that, but I believe that goes against the culture here. If one does want to go forward, that behavior would probably have to change or there would have to be a massive change in the corporate culture—one I feel is still a long time away.

The more support you have from all quarters, the more flexible you can be. Acknowledging your partner's and your coworkers' needs will get you more support from them. "When I have an impending deadline, I might work sixty to eighty hours a week," says Richard, who works full time in a home office, and whose wife, Janine, works full time outside the home. "Then Janine will cover those hours for me—or vice versa, when she has extra pressure at work. We have to negotiate, sharing and supporting each other. Balancing is always both people's problem. It's a classic 'getting to yes.' "

Even in a company that has come to understand the need to support flexibility, things don't stay put. Staff or top management changes can result in backsliding, and the dialogue must begin again. "We got a new executive director about two and a half years ago, a very rigid, very tradition-oriented guy," says Kate. "He wanted to have his main management meeting every Monday morning at eight o'clock, but one of the other directors said, 'Hey, that's not the kind of institution we are. We try to be sensitive to the needs of families. Can we make it later?' And everybody agreed we would meet at nine o'clock. Nine o'clock was do-able."

Rigid, tradition-oriented management will probably always be with us, and today's job market, with its emphasis on lean-mean management, is increasingly difficult. As Fred notes, "Many employers will just keep handing employees work and demanding a lot and unless they say no, no one's going to tell them, 'Oh, stop. You're doing too much.' I think the trend in a lot of corporate workplaces is asking people to do more because of downsizing. It's as if they're saying, 'We kept you. Now you've got to do more.' "

We are still a long way from a family-friendly workplace or a family-friendly culture. The kind of flexibility that enables parents to balance work and family responsibilities is emerging in some organizations, but it will take a lot of commitment and energy to make it widely available. "The bottom line is that nothing is perfect," says Sherrie. "You have to work out the best possible compromise for you and your kids. Every step of the way is making choices. Choose your battles."

Notes

1. B. P. Noble, "Now He's Stressed, She's Stressed," *New York Times*, October 9, 1994.
2. B. Olmsted and S. Smith, *Creating a Flexible Workplace*, 2d ed. (New York: AMACOM, 1994).
3. L. Bailyn, *Breaking the Mold: Women, Men and Time in the New Corporate World* (New York: Free Press, 1993), p. 109.

8

Negotiating Shared Roles

by Leah Potts Fisher and Chris Essex
of The Center for Work and the Family

> We had a revolution in the role of women without a revolution in
> the role of men or in the institutions which most define them
> both—the family and the workplace. Capitalism has incorporated
> mothers into wage work while ignoring the needs of families and
> while exerting pressure on men to stay as they have been.
>
> —Arlie Hochschild, *Swarthmore College Bulletin,*
> February 1991

How often have you and your partner fallen into bed at 11:30 or
midnight or later, after returning from full-time jobs to care for
your home and children, and either thought or said aloud to each
other, "I can't believe we are going to get up in just six more hours
and do this all over again!"

Many couples today find themselves caught in the midst of a
crisis in caretaking. As a result of women's entry into the paid

The Center for Work and the Family, founded in 1990 in Berkeley, California, designs and
delivers innovative programs for work and family integration. Professional Lives/Personal
Lives: Finding a Balance, The Effects of Business Travel on Relationships and Family Life,
Coping Strategies for Work/Family Stress, Weekend Couples' Retreats for Managers, and
Workplace Parenting Groups are examples of services designed to help employees achieve
satisfaction in both their professional and personal lives. Center programs include a unique
feature: Following day-long seminars, a feedback briefing is offered to management. An
overview of the training program is presented along with feedback and recommendations
from seminar participants. Center services are available privately and through the workplace. For information, contact The Center for Work and the Family, 910 Tulare Avenue,
Berkeley, CA 94707, (510) 527-0107.

labor force without accompanying social changes, working men and women find themselves lacking the time or energy to give the care and nurturing they wish to give to their children, their homes, and their relationships. Attempting to deal with this collision of work and family demands without benefit of a broader social perspective can lead to hurt and anger between husbands and wives that erupt in misunderstandings like these:

- If I'm this overworked and overwhelmed, you must not be doing your share.
- If we're both working this hard and struggling, surely we must be doing something wrong.
- If I feel this criticized, disregarded, and uncared for by my partner, I must be with the wrong person.

Sometimes these perceptions are accurate; there are partners who do far less than their fair share at home. More often, the perceptions are the emotional residue of too much stress created by work and family demands, too few resources to address them, and a lack of communication skills for dealing with the resulting conflicts.

How easily our partner can come to feel like the enemy. "In looking for explanations, we tend to see what is in our line of vision," observes author and clinician Lillian Rubin, Ph.D.[1] An exhausted mom at the end of the day sees her husband sitting in front of the television; an overworked and overwhelmed husband comes home to find his wife on the telephone chatting with a friend and the house untidy. Neither sees the indirect forces that contribute to their exhaustion, leaving both in need of care. Neither identifies the source of problems as a society that portrays itself as pro-family yet fails to supply its citizens with adequate day care, health care, quality education, sick-child care, or—until recently—parental leave. Confusion reigns because men and women are overwhelmed with balancing work and family and don't understand why.

Women are confused by feeling resentful and guilty simultaneously—resentful for doing the bulk of the work at home on top of their paid employment, guilty about spending less time with their children than their own mothers did.

Men, too, are confused. They compare themselves to their fathers and know that they're doing far more caretaking than the previous generation of men, yet their wives tell them they are being unfair and not doing enough at home. Today's "good father" is expected to be actively involved at home, yet no less is expected of him at work.

Finally, couples argue over who does what and what is fair as they try to meet the needs of children and household without the presence of an adult at home during the day.

What couples tend to argue over most is the distribution of household chores and child care tasks. But underneath those arguments may lie deeper issues of isolation, loss of intimacy, feelings of resentment, exhaustion, stress, depression, disconnection, and fear of divorce.

This chapter is designed to help couples renegotiate household labor. But first a word of caution: Even if you faithfully follow every suggestion and complete every exercise, the problem of excessive, competing demands will not go away. We hope you will be able to communicate and cope better until much-needed social changes occur. Throughout, you need to keep reminding yourself: "This is our problem, but it is not our fault."

Preparing to Negotiate

Preparing to negotiate involves three tasks for couples: making a commitment to examine your current relationship, identifying your unmet needs, and analyzing the current division of labor.

Commitment to Examining the Relationship

It is not uncommon for one or both partners to feel threatened at the prospect of bringing up the topic of shared roles. Each is probably feeling overworked, resentful, and misunderstood, so this is a hot topic.

Often one partner is more eager than the other to examine the relationship. Reticence may stem from fear of being blamed, guilt, fear of change, and concern that the relationship cannot survive this much scrutiny.

If your partner resists your efforts to examine the relationship, try these strategies:

❑ Spend some time alone together doing enjoyable things. This activity helps create a reservoir of goodwill. For working couples with children, scheduling intimate time together may seem like just one more chore, but it is a wise investment, especially in the challenging task ahead.

❑ Approach the task positively as a win-win situation. Help your partner understand that working together for greater happiness in the relationship will benefit both of you and your children.

❑ Try saying "please." Faced with resistance, we often overlook this common courtesy and instead are argumentative and accusatory.

❑ Agree on a time limit after which you will seek consultation, counseling, or mediation if you haven't succeeded in addressing these issues on your own.

❑ If the time limit passes, make an appointment to see a counselor. Be forewarned: Once an appointment has been made, there is a tendency for couples to be on their best behavior and then decide to cancel the appointment. Resist the urge to cancel.

❑ Don't be surprised if, after the resistant partner agrees to examine the relationship, the more willing partner experiences an increased level of resistance. The status quo, however problematic, is familiar to both of you.

Identifying Unmet Needs

Paradoxically the first steps in working as a team to negotiate shared roles are individual ones. Separately, we need to examine our own needs, the tasks described in detail in Chapters 2 and 6. In this chapter, we'll look at how clarifying our own needs is helpful in negotiating with our partner.

Here's a scenario: Bert walks in the front door later than usual after a particularly horrible commute. He leaves his briefcase in the hallway and walks into the kitchen. Baby Gretchen is playing on the floor with pots and pans; his wife, Nancy, is in the adjoining room, engrossed in painting at her easel. There is clutter everywhere and no sign of dinner. Bert counts to ten. He knows if he opens his mouth right away, nothing good will come from it.

Feelings about unfairness, resentment, indignation, and envy can provide us with valuable clues about our own unmet needs. However, we often either dismiss these feelings as immature or act on them impulsively, often with negative consequences. Instead of suppressing or blasting, Bert would do well to ask himself, "What is this fury trying to tell me? What besides dinner might I need that I'm not aware of?" This internal process lays the groundwork for later effective communication. Bert's self-reflection, for example, may lead him to realize that he too needs some decompression time when he first gets home.

Liz, a union negotiator for the teachers' union, is on a year's maternity leave. She describes intense anger and envy of her husband, whose life appears to have changed remarkably little with the birth of their daughter, whereas her life has changed dramatically and seemingly forever. If she expresses her envy and resentment as raw snappishness and complaint, it's likely to result only in confusion and distance. What is behind these intense feelings? Does Liz want acknowledgment of how much her life has changed? Does she want reassurance that she'll have her husband's active support at home next year when she returns to work? Does she yearn for more equitable sharing of tasks now so she can plan to return to her former life more quickly? Or does she simply need a little additional time to herself for recreation or rest? Her negotiation with her husband will depend on what she decides she really needs.

Finding personal answers to these not-so-simple questions must come first and will be critical to the success of any couple's negotiations that may come later. Bert and Liz need to identify the personal needs that are buried under their anger, resentment, or envy.

Another significant threat to successful negotiation is a perception that our partner is the primary source of our overwhelmed condition. Any hard-working and well-intentioned partner, whether or not he or she is doing an equal share of the work at home, will resent the accusation, "You are unfair" or "You are not doing enough." Resentment begets more resentment, and partners may begin to draw apart and keep their distance. It is essential for working couples to redirect their attention to what each partner is giving the other, to remind themselves of the larger social context, and to see each other as potential allies facing a challenging problem. The focus on appreciation starts a positive spiral. Appreciation begets more appreciation.

There's a crucial relationship between caring and caretaking, but for some partners it is hard to see the connection between love and housework. "Of course I love her. What does changing diapers or washing dishes have to do with love?" asks an exasperated husband. Yet wives commonly describe feeling loved and cared for when spouses actively engage in housework and child care, particularly if husbands initiate such caretaking activity without being asked or reminded. Carolyn and Philip Cowan, directors of the Becoming a Family Project at the University of California and authors of *When Partners Become Parents: The Big Life Change for Couples,* have examined how the division of labor affects new parents' marital satisfaction. Tanya, who participated in the Cowans' Becoming a Family Project, says,"When I see Jackson making an extra effort with Kevin, I feel that he's telling me he loves me. Rationally, I know that he and Kevin have their own thing going, but it makes me feel so good about him. And when we were fighting because Jackson wasn't really doing anything with Kevin, that just felt like a slap in my face."[2]

Sociologist Arlie Hochschild refers to "an economy of gratitude" as "the summary of all felt gifts." "In the light of changing cultural ideas about manhood and womanhood, what does a wife expect from her husband? What does she take as a gift, and so feel moved to thank him for? What does he want to be thanked for? What really feels to the husband like a gift from her? Is the gift she wants to give the one he wants to receive?"[3]

Because caring is expressed differently by different people, it is important for you and your partner to identify what makes each of you feel cared for and what you are doing to show care and affection.

Here is an exercise designed to help you reinforce an upward spiral of gratitude and appreciation. You and your partner should complete Worksheet 1 separately and then discuss your responses with each other. It can provide you with valuable information and insights into the "gifts" in your relationship.

Spending time together as a couple, identifying unmet needs, and recognizing the gifts you exchange in your relationship all can help partners feel more like allies and less like competitors. The goal is to remain allies in dealing with a complex social problem rather than become competitors for the scarce resources of time, money, or rest.

Worksheet 1:
Caring and Appreciation

How do you and your partner show your appreciation for each other? How do you demonstrate that you care? A "gift" is a demonstration of caring and love. Examples of "gifts" have included: "A special dinner," "She listens to me," and "He kills bugs for me."

1. What are some "gifts" your partner gives you or your family which you appreciate? _____

_____

_____

_____

2. What are some of the "gifts" you wish your partner would give to you or your family? _____

_____

_____

_____

3. What "gifts" do you give your partner or family which he/she seems to appreciate? _____

_____

_____

_____

4. Are there "gifts" you give to your partner or family which he/she does not seem to notice or appreciate? _____

_____

_____

_____

5. Are there discrepancies between you and your partner in what is thought of as a "gift" (given or received) and what is thought to be an expectation of shared roles? If yes, what is an example? ___

_____

_____

_____

Source: The Center for Work and the Family, copyright © 1993.

Examining the Division of Labor

You have one more step before negotiating shared roles: Each of you needs to examine independently how you divide the labor in your household. A prerequisite for any negotiation is seeing clearly how things are currently and how you want them to be. Each partner needs to ask:

- What am I contributing to the care of my household and family?
- How do I feel about it?
- What do I like and wish to keep the way it is?
- What would I like to change?
- Why do I want these changes?

In their Becoming a Family Project, the Cowans found that in marriages where fathers were actively involved with household tasks and child care, both partners felt greater satisfaction in the marriage. The Cowans also found that partners who were satisfied with the division of tasks, regardless of the details of the division, had significantly greater personal and marital satisfaction. Perhaps the process of mutually determining the division of labor affects satisfaction with the arrangement. Deciding together who does what helps couples feel like collaborators.

The Cowans developed several useful instruments for measuring who does what. Try one or more of these exercises; each elicits different information and addresses a different aspect of family life.

Worksheet 2, "Who Does What? 1" examines the distribution of labor for meals, laundry, and general home care. Do the exercise separately; then share your responses.

As you share your responses, you may be surprised to realize how much your partner actually does, or you may both discover that things are truly out of balance. You may be unhappy about the discrepancies between the "how it is now" and the "how I would like it to be" columns, or relieved by the similarities. It is likely that the two of you may have different perceptions about how much you're doing. Note these differences in perception.

It is common to be more aware of what we ourselves are doing to support and care for home and family and less aware of what our partner is doing. The Cowans discovered that "each claims to

Worksheet 2:
Who Does What? 1

Please show how you and your partner divide the family tasks listed here. Using the numbers on the scale below, show **HOW IT IS NOW** down the left side and **HOW I WOULD LIKE IT TO BE** down the right side.

1	2	3	4	5	6	7	8	9
she does it all				we both do this about equally			**he** does it all	

HOW IT IS NOW		HOW I WOULD LIKE IT TO BE
	A. Planning and preparing meals	
	B. Cleaning up after meals	
	C. Repairs around the home	
	D. Housecleaning	
	E. Taking out the garbage	
	F. Buying groceries, household needs	
	G. Paying bills	
	H. Laundry: washing, folding, ironing	
	I. Writing letters/making calls to family and friends	
	J. Looking after the car	
	K. Providing income for our family	
	L. Caring for plants, garden, yard	
	M. Working outside the family	

Worksheet 2 (continued)

    N. In general, how satisfied are you with the way you and your partner divide the family tasks?

☐ Very   ☐ Pretty   ☐ Neutral   ☐ Somewhat   ☐ Very
   Satisfied   Satisfied   Dissatisfied   Dissatisfied

    O. In general, how satisfied are you with the way you and your partner divide the work outside the family?

☐ Very   ☐ Pretty   ☐ Neutral   ☐ Somewhat   ☐ Very
   Satisfied   Satisfied   Dissatisfied   Dissatisfied

Source: Copyright © 1978, 1990 by Carolyn Pape Cowan and Philip A. Cowan, Becoming a Family Project, University of California at Berkeley.

be doing more than the other ever gives him credit for. The feeling of not being appreciated for the endless amount of work each partner actually does undoubtedly increases tension between them." If there are differences in perception, try to avoid arguing about whose perspective is the truth. Your perceptions don't have to be the same to negotiate change successfully.

Look at "how it is now." Think about how these patterns got established. Did they make good sense at one time but no longer? One mother, for example, happily did most of the child care and all the household chores while she was home with the baby for three years. However, the "baby" is 5 years old now, she has been working full time for two years, and she is still doing all the cleaning, cooking, shopping, and planning. Her first reaction was resentment at an arrangement that she felt was unfair and unequal. Then she realized that she and her husband were overdue for a renegotiation of household duties.

As you answer the "how I would like it to be" column in all these exercises, think about why you want this change and why it matters to you. One father, for example, discovered he resented doing dishes because it meant being left alone in the kitchen after dinner; a mother realized she preferred to wash and fold her own laundry because she is very particular about it, but she wanted her partner's help in putting it away; another mother wanted her partner's participation in visiting and choosing preschools, because the decision felt to her like such a momentous one.

Often in conversations about shared roles, the word "unfair" comes up. Negotiating who does what as a moral issue is almost guaranteed to put one's partner on the defensive. Inequality may, in fact, be a real issue, but it is never the whole issue. What feels unfair? The amount of household labor each performs? The amount of discretionary time each partner has? Or inequity in the amount of influence each partner has over decision making?

Couples may be using their persistent conflicts over housework and child care chores as a way of trying to communicate about the deeper, less tangible issue of how much power and influence each has in the relationship. Identifying how much influence each partner feels she or he has over family decisions is the goal of the exercise in Worksheet 3.

The exercise in Worksheet 4 considers who does what in daily care for a baby.

The final exercise, the household task analysis in Worksheet 5, asks you to identify specific chores and to consider them from a number of angles. An understanding of why you want support, help, or relief from certain tasks will predispose you to communicate with your partner in "I" statements instead of "you" statements. "I" statements make you take responsibility for your own feelings, needs, and opinions; statements that begin with "you" often are blaming and critical, and they tend to be perceived as attacks and elicit defensiveness. Compare, for example, "I hate the helpless feeling of calling one busy teenager after another looking for a sitter. Please share this task," with, "It's unfair that you leave all the sitter arrangements to me, since we both want to go out."

In sharing your responses to the household task analysis (Worksheet 5) with your partner, you may make some interesting discoveries. Your partner may be more willing to help once he or she understands the reason behind your request; you may want to swap chores if one of you hates a task the other doesn't mind doing; you may be relieved of guilt about not assisting with a chore your partner actually wants to have total control over. And you may decide to rotate or hire out the chores you both detest.

Creating and nurturing relationships that are respectful and egalitarian is difficult. We have few role models. But what are we striving for? What does equality mean in marriage? Here are some ideas.

Worksheet 3:
Who Does What? 2

Please show how much influence you and your partner have in the family decisions listed here. Using the numbers on the scale below, show **HOW IT IS NOW** down the left side and **HOW I WOULD LIKE IT TO BE** down the right side.

1	2	3	4	5	6	7	8	9
she does it all				we both do this about equally			**he** does it all	

HOW IT IS NOW		HOW I WOULD LIKE IT TO BE
	A. Deciding how we spend time at home	
	B. Deciding how we spend time out of the house	
	C. Deciding which friends and family to see, and when	
	D. Deciding about vacation: when, where, expenses	
	E. Deciding about major expenses: house, car, furniture	
	F. Deciding about financial planning: insurance, loans, taxes, plans for saving, etc.	
	G. Deciding when and how much time both partners should work outside the family	
	H. Initiating lovemaking	
	I. Determining the frequency of lovemaking	
	J. Deciding about religious practices in our family	
	K. Deciding about involvement in community activities	
	L. Deciding how people should behave toward one another in our family	

M. In general, how satisfied are you with the way you and your partner divide the family decisions?

☐ Very   ☐ Pretty   ☐ Neutral   ☐ Somewhat   ☐ Very
satisfied   satisfied   dissatisfied   dissatisfied

N. In your relationship with your partner, who would you say has the influence in decision making?

☐ Woman has more   ☐ Man has more   ☐ We have about
                                                 equal influence

O. In the relationship between your parents, who would you say had the influence in decision making?

☐ Woman had more   ☐ Man had more   ☐ They had about
                                                 equal influence

---

Source: Copyright © 1978, 1990 by Carolyn Pape Cowan and Philip A. Cowan, Becoming a Family Project, University of California at Berkeley.

In egalitarian relationships, both partners have equal ownership of their life together; they have equal amounts of influence over the large and small decisions that affect them both. It may mean equal amounts of discretionary time and money. It certainly means equal respect for each other's needs and wishes.

There are some caveats about working toward an egalitarian relationship. It is necessary to trust your partner's goodwill—something that comes more easily to some individuals than to others. A partner who is afraid of being overpowered or disregarded may have trouble compromising, taking turns, or staying with the hard work of reaching agreement. A person who appears to disregard his or her partner's needs and feelings, or refuses to confront or communicate about problems, or tries to seize power through intimidation may also be a person who feels in danger of being disregarded, overpowered, or bullied. If inequities are long-standing and both partners feel vulnerable, they will probably need professional mediation or counseling to make meaningful changes.

Though difficult to learn, nothing leaves partners feeling safer, sexier, more romantic, or more intimate than the knowledge that they will be treated with respect and that they are equals in making

(Text continues on page 138.)

Worksheet 4:
Who Does What? 3

On this page we ask you about 3 aspects of caring for <u>your first child</u>. Using the numbers on our 1 to 9 scale, show **HOW IT IS NOW** and **HOW I WOULD LIKE IT TO BE.**

1	2	3	4	5	6	7	8	9
she does it all				we both do this about equally			**he** does it all	

*In the farthest right column, show how competent you feel—that is, how much you feel you do each of these tasks well—using the 1 to 5 scale for competence below.

5	4	3	2	1
Very competent		Moderately competent		Not at all competent

HOW IT IS NOW (1 to 9)		**HOW I WOULD LIKE IT TO BE** (1 to 9)	**HOW COMPETENT I FEEL DOING THIS** (1 to 5)
	A. Reading to our child		
	B. Preparing meals for our child		
	C. Dressing our child		
	D. Cleaning or bathing our child		
	E. Deciding whether or how to respond to our child's crying		
	F. Getting up at night with our child		
	G. Taking our child out: drives, parks, walks, visits, playgrounds		

HOW IT IS NOW (1 to 9)		HOW I WOULD LIKE IT TO BE (1 to 9)	HOW COMPETENT I FEEL DOING THIS (1 to 5)
	H. Choosing toys for our child		
	I. Playing with our child		
	J. Doing our child's laundry		
	K. Arranging for babysitters or child care		
	L. Dealing with the doctor regarding our child's health		
	M. Getting our child to and from school		
	N. Tending to our child in public: restaurants, visiting, shopping, playgrounds		
	O. Setting limits for our child		
	P. Disciplining our child		
	Q. Teaching our child		
	R. Picking up after our child		
	S. Arranging our child's visits, play with friends		
	T. Helping when our child has a problem with playmates/siblings		

Source: Copyright © 1978, 1990 by Carolyn Pape Cowan and Philip A. Cowan, Becoming a Family Project, University of California at Berkeley.

Worksheet 5:
Household Task Analysis

Think about all the chores, tasks, and activities you have done in the past few weeks in caring for your home, children, and family. It may be helpful to list these activities and tasks on a separate piece of paper. Can you identify one or more tasks that fit the following categories?

1. I do these activities/tasks myself because I enjoy them; they give me pleasure and satisfaction:

_____

_____

_____

2. I do these activities/tasks myself because I want them done a certain way (i.e., I want control over how they are done or I want to be sure they are done to a certain standard):

_____

_____

_____

3. I do these activities/tasks because I think I *should* be the one to do them:

_____

_____

_____

4. I do not mind doing these activities/tasks, but I would like to do them less often:

_____

_____

_____

5. I *hate* doing these tasks!

_____

_____

_____

6. These are tasks I never get around to, and I would like help to address them:

_____

_____

_____

7. These are tasks I'd like to do with my partner because I am unsure of myself, I am uncertain about how to proceed, or they make me anxious:

_____

_____

_____

8. If someone would show me how, in a supportive way, I would be willing to get more involved with these tasks/activities:

_____

_____

_____

9. These are tasks that I wish we as a couple would agree to do less often or less perfectly:

_____

_____

_____

Source: The Center for Work and the Family, copyright © 1993.

decisions about matters affecting their life together. The exercises in this chapter, completed at whatever pace is best for you, will be good preparation for beginning your negotiation of shared roles.

Negotiation of Change: A Ten-Step Approach

This step-by-step procedure is designed to help you negotiate the division of labor in your partnership. You will probably need to renegotiate roles and responsibilities periodically as you move through the changes of the life cycle: marriage, a career change, childbirth, return to work, a child's entry into school, and others. If conflict over shared roles is symptomatic of deeper issues, this procedure may be a useful beginning, but most likely it will not be sufficient to sustain lasting change.

Step 1: Identify Your Unmet Needs

This first step is a private one of self-reflection. What important needs are going unmet? Do you need time alone? Time with your partner? Exercise? Lovemaking? These unmet needs may be the heat beneath fights about housework. Anger, resentment, and a sense of unfairness are useful as signals to yourself about unmet needs. They are not useful as negotiating tools.

Step 2: Create a Time to Discuss Important Issues
and Set an Agenda

Don't try to negotiate in the heat of anger. You want to have your partner's best attention, so set aside a time without interruptions. You might even want to make an appointment. Parents of young children may need to arrange for a sitter and go out. Some couples believe that marriage should be more spontaneous than this and find the idea of making an appointment unromantic. But there is a place for being businesslike in romance; it can go a long way toward preventing "spontaneous" chaos, confusion, and fury.

Couples need time for both short-term and long-term planning. A weekly meeting is helpful to clarify and coordinate schedules and to delegate chores. An annual meeting or weekend retreat to review lifetime dreams and do long-range planning is also valuable.

Step 3: Communicate Your Needs and Feelings Without Blame

Communicate your feelings and your needs, but avoid accusation and blame. "I'm feeling so overwhelmed." "I'm feeling lonely." "I feel unappreciated." Expressing yourself angrily can derail these negotiations. Be prepared to listen respectfully to your partner's feelings. Remember: "I feel you are selfish and unfair" is not a feeling; it's a judgment.

Step 4: Include Your Partner in the Process

Keep the attitude: What are *we* going to do about these responsibilities? Many people confuse needs with solutions. "I need you to come home earlier" is not a need. It is a proposed solution, and by no means the only one. Needs begin with "I"; they refer to the self. Here's an example: "I realize I get overwhelmed between 5:30 and 7:30 at night when I'm home alone with the kids. I need help. What can we do about this?" You have included your partner in the planning process and avoided a struggle over a single proposed solution.

If your partner is resistant or forgetful, don't give up. Keep coming back to the planning table. Have regular meetings. Recognize the scope of our challenge: redefining the roles of men and women. Expect meaningful changes to take time.

Step 5: Identify a Specific Issue to Negotiate

Start small. Select a manageable task to begin with or a small part of a long-standing or highly emotional concern. For example, try negotiating who will cook and clean up after Tuesday dinners instead of taking on all the family meals. Your successes will encourage you to tackle more complex problems.

Step 6: Brainstorm Possible Solutions

Look for more than one possible solution so you don't get caught up in debating or arguing about a single solution. Consider a variety of ways to meet your identified needs. Remember not to confuse needs with solutions. "I need you to . . ." is not a need; it is a single solution. Generate multiple solutions together.

Step 7: Identify Resources

Look around for additional sources of help to meet your needs. It is common for couples to get into the habit of "seesaw" thinking: "If you won't do it, then I have to." Who else might be able to help? Other possibilities include work exchanges, enlisting older children to do more, or purchasing household help or take-out meals.

Step 8: Select One Strategy

Once you've agreed on a new strategy, be as specific as possible about how it will be implemented. Let's say you have reached an agreement about how you'll equitably handle the event of a sick child; now anticipate and work out the details. For example, "When a child is sick, we'll alternate staying home unless one of us has an important meeting or is out of town. If we both have important commitments, we will hire a sick-child care service. The partner whose turn it is will be responsible for calling the service and making the arrangements."

Step 9: Set a Time to Evaluate the New Arrangement and to Renegotiate, If Necessary

Try out the new arrangement for a specified time. What parts worked well? What didn't work? What modifications are needed? Decide together if you'll adopt the new arrangement, modify it, or negotiate a different one.

Step 10: Express Appreciation

Take time to notice and acknowledge what your partner is doing for the family, even if further changes are needed. Tell your partner what you want to be appreciated for. Remember to reinforce an upward spiral of appreciation rather than a downward spiral of resentment.

If Your Negotiations Get Stuck

If you and your partner attempt to negotiate changes in household arrangements—you've read this chapter, done the exercises, tried the strategies—and you are still unsuccessful, consider these three actions:

1. Go back and be sure you really followed the ten-step negotiation procedures. Old habits are hard to break. Have you set aside adequate time to discuss the arrangements you want to change? Are you separating needs from solutions? Are you refraining from blame? Are you brainstorming solutions together? Have you given it a long enough trial? A minimum of two weeks is a good idea for trying out any new arrangement. You or your partner may still be expecting the same old painful responses; you will need time to test whether the sarcasm, criticism, or procrastination is really gone. Have you continued to meet regularly, or are you trying to accomplish this change in a single meeting?

2. Ask yourself about mixed motives and hidden agendas. What is your objective in negotiating with your partner? Are you truly trying to achieve better balance in caring for your family and home? Or might you also be tempted to use this opportunity to vent your anger over past hurts and injustices? Are you inclined to assert your moral superiority as a parent or a homemaker or a mellow guy? Do you feel compelled to defend yourself against expected accusations of being neglectful, unfair, uncaring, or otherwise unworthy of respect, love, and intimacy?

   Such feelings are completely understandable and need to be talked about, but they should be reserved for a different time. If you are trying to negotiate changes, hidden agendas can derail the process. For example, a husband says to his wife, "I wish you would understand how hard I am working and help me learn to be better organized."

Defensively, his wife breaks in, "Well, I wish you'd appreciate how hard *I'm* working. Just going to the market with two little kids is an ordeal!" The negotiation and collaboration have been interrupted, and the couple's focus shifts to a competition over who has the harder life.

3. Be alert to the possibility of unrecognized conflicts. When couples cannot reach decisions about home care and child care despite earnest attempts, when they cannot agree on a concept of fairness despite goodwill and a strong desire to do so, then their relationship is probably being affected by some conflict about which they are unaware. This is the area that most often requires professional intervention.

How do you know when this is the case? There is a subtle boundary between household chore wars as their own legitimate issue and household conflicts that are symptomatic of other conflicts. In the former case, couples tend to be open to solutions that meet their needs. They accept practical suggestions, respond to invitations for greater intimacy, arrive more quickly at new arrangements, and are more willing to use outside resources. When chore wars are symptomatic of underlying issues, however, one or both partners may continue to struggle, blame, accuse, attack, or resist. They refuse to take the discussion to a deeper level. Housework is a club to bludgeon or be bludgeoned with; it is justification for criticism and contempt. These couples need help distinguishing the anger that accompanies an unfair arrangement from the fury that hints at some additional unrecognized issue.

Individuals may be covering up a variety of feelings, concerns, or conflicts in their repetitive fights over sharing chores. Here are some examples:

- Unrecognized, unmet needs, especially the need and desire to be taken care of
- Anxiety about loss of control or autonomy
- Concerns about closeness and distance
- Concerns about gender roles—unresolved issues about being a working parent and a good mother or

good father; what it means to be a good man or good woman

What's Going On Beneath the Surface of Constant Conflict?

Impediments to successful couples' negotiations can take the form of avoidance, resistance, or overt conflict.

If disagreement makes either or both partners anxious, they may resort to avoidance rather than confront their partner's intense feelings or their own. Such individuals cope with their anxiety by keeping away from certain areas and preventing intimate communication from taking place. A banker and his wife describe their avoidance this way: "We don't exactly have chore wars. With us it's more like cold war." They live with tension and silent resentment, steering clear of certain topics lest an eruption occur. The wife comments poignantly, "We can't seem to talk about managing our household finances without a fight, so we just don't discuss it. My husband talks to people all day long about money, but we can't ever discuss it."

The resistant style might look like this: Sally resents the fact that she does most of the care of their baby, though both she and her husband are working. Sally nags and Joe alternates between procrastinating, doing family chores badly, and forgetting. The more Sally nags, the less Joe participates. Sally becomes more and more angry, critical, and self-righteous. Asked to explain his lack of involvement, Joe says, "I slow down because I don't want to encourage that kind of nagging from Sally."

Complaints or confrontation can arouse anxiety and lead to resistance as a pattern of response. If the interaction is experienced as an attack rather than an effort at problem solving, the partner may offer resistance. Common forms of resistance include denying responsibility—"It wasn't my fault!"—and countercomplaints—"But what about the time you did the same thing?"

When overt conflict or "uproar" occurs, it may represent failed attempts at avoidance or resistance. This was frequently the result when the banker's wife pressured her husband to talk about household finances. It also can be a strategy for warding off anxiety about too much closeness. Getting in a fight and stomping out can be a way for one or both partners to get space. Angry outbursts also may represent clumsy attempts to communicate about other, more vulnerable emotions such as hurt or sadness. Sally's outbursts about household chores and baby care distracted her as well as Joe from the underlying sadness she felt about the loss of marital intimacy since the birth of their baby.

For men in particular, a wide range of emotions may get filtered through the emotion of anger. Joe observes, "When I feel hurt or sad, it comes across as anger. I don't even know right away that I'm hurt or sad. I just feel mad! To admit that you're hurt is to admit that you are weak, and men aren't supposed to be weak."

When caring, committed couples cannot seem to make any headway in renegotiating the care of home and children, when every effort ends up in avoidance, resistance, or uproar, they would be wise to wonder about deeper issues at the core of their impasse.

Getting Additional Help

What kind of support do couples need if they cannot renegotiate shared roles by themselves? Possible sources of help are parent education classes, support groups for mothers or fathers, parenting or couples groups, pastoral counseling, marital counseling, or psychotherapy. Support groups can help working parents realize how normal the conflicts they face are. With professional support, couples can become more aware of their own and their partner's needs. Each partner can be helped to see the validity of the other person's view. Partners can learn to communicate more directly about what they need, feel, and want. They can learn to negotiate openly for power, intimacy, and space rather than hide these needs under other issues. In addition, they can try out new patterns of behavior, with opportunities to practice and discuss them.

Changing patterns means facing the unfamiliar. Getting angry and fighting can be a way of avoiding change, or a way of consoling yourself when you are convinced nothing will ever change. Counseling can provide the safety to pace changes, to evaluate and discuss them, and to examine the feelings that emerge with each change.

"But my partner won't go" is a frequently voiced concern. Be sure you've asked your partner explicitly and politely. Do not assume that he or she won't go. Classes or groups may be less threatening than therapy. If you must, go alone and pave the way for involving your partner. Propose going with your partner for a consultation. You can meet with a counselor without deciding to enter ongoing therapy. Use the consultation to determine if outside help is appropriate, to get a better understanding of what the counseling might entail, and to decide if you want to work with this particular professional.

What Is It All for?

This chapter has offered strategies to help couples cope with a national crisis in caretaking—the problems that arise from the social, economic, and labor force changes that have upset the old balance whereby men worked outside the home for pay and shared their earnings with women who did the domestic caretaking. The slow response of workplaces and government has left the family to be the shock absorber for systems that don't flex easily.

In creating new arrangements at work and home that correspond to new realities, couples are challenged to cope with caretaking fairly and equitably, and in ways that are meaningful to each partner and to the family as a whole. In the corporate world, joint managerial relationships are among the most challenging to establish and sustain. That is precisely what men and women are attempting to do in the home.

Whatever arrangement a couple arrives at, it will feel best if it has been mutually negotiated. As individuals, as couples, and as families, we are paving new pathways in clarifying the roles of men and women at work and at home. We can take comfort from the fact that our efforts should ease the way for our sons and daughters as they enter the workforce of the future.

Notes

1. Lillian B. Rubin, *Families on the Faultline: American Working Class Speaks About the Family, the Economy, Race, and Ethnicity* (New York: Harper Perennial, 1995).
2. Carolyn Pape Cowan and Philip A. Cowan, *When Partners Become Parents: The Big Life Change for Couples* (New York: Basic Books, 1992), p. 102.
3. Arlie Hochschild, "The Economy of Gratitude," in David Franks and Doyle McCarthy, eds., *Original Papers in the Sociology of Emotions* (Greenwich, Conn.: JAI Press, 1989).

9

Building Networks for Social and Practical Support

You need to be public with your family; you need to go out and develop that sense of community so that the child understands that he belongs to a nuclear family but he also belongs to a broader family.

—Lena, married, part-time health care consultant,
one child, age 3

Most of the people we interviewed who were relatively happy with their work-family balance found support from other people to be a major contributor to their family harmony. By luck or through dedicated effort, they've found extended family or community to sustain them in their efforts to care for their children while supporting their families economically. To some, creating social support came naturally and easily. Others were brought to it by necessity. Those who emphasized social support included men and women, people in couples, and single parents. They said that their support networks reduced their stress, or at least helped them to cope with stress with fewer negative consequences.

Fred, his wife Elizabeth, and their two children moved recently, a change that reinforced the value of counting on other people. "What helps," Fred reflects, "are people you can call when you're stuck somewhere and need your kids picked up or where you can drop them off in the morning when you need to leave early. We've had that where we were living, and we'll develop a similar network where we are now. That circle means a lot. I feel very close to all the parents, though if I met them on their own, without the kids, we might not have found all that much in common."

Support is crucial for every day, and even more essential in times of crisis. "There's one school couple that we know well," said Kate. "I've called them, and I've taken their girls a few times. I had an operation last fall, and one of the parents found out about it and said, 'You're not going to be able to pick up Claire, so let me pick her up. She can spend the night. You can rest and have the evening alone.' It was just that: knowing enough about people's lives to be able to help out."

The need for social support is particularly important for single parents. "When my son was little, social support was, plain and simple, the way we survived and the way we prospered," observes Alice.

The value of social support, according to our interviewees, extended to the children as well as to the parents. They felt that their children benefited from the stimulation of knowing a variety of people and from the security of being able to rely on people other than their parents. Several found that their children developed strong peer relationships over time, similar in quality to those with cousins or other relatives, with children who were part of their families' community of support. They felt that their children were nourished and sustained by these relationships.

Barriers to Mobilizing Social Support

To create good support systems requires recognizing and overcoming numerous barriers, internal and external. It is important to understand the social and collective aspects of many of these barriers. Otherwise developing a good social support system can easily become another "should" by which we measure our worth. "A good working parent should have time to develop a functional, pleasant support network after working all day and racing home to take care of the children." Or "It's my fault if I don't have time or energy to change this part of my life." Of course, life might work better if you had more and better-quality support. On the other hand, you may be too overwhelmed to imagine how to create support, or you might face real limitations that prevent you from converting wishes to realities. It is usually possible—and sometimes a necessity—to create strong support systems. But parents need to support each other in this process.

Here are some of the barriers you might face in trying to create a support system:

- A sense that asking for help places you in a "one-down," needy, defensive, pathetic position. Many people believe they should be able to handle work and family and anything else that comes along, alone and unaided. "Look at all those other people. They're doing fine. What's the matter with me?" (This issue is discussed further in Chapter 10.)

- The desire to appear strong, together, on top of it. "If I tell anyone how I really feel, they'll know I'm a failure." Even if you don't think you're a failure, you might fear that telling people the truth about your limits and vulnerabilities will cause them to lower their opinions of you. That might be true.

- The desire not to appear too strong, together, or on top of it, which can prevent us from talking openly about the happy, successful parts of our lives. This reticence limits our ability to create honest relationships. "It's not socially acceptable not to feel torn about work and family," says Catherine. "If I'm at a party and meet other mothers and they find out I'm working, they say, 'Oh, that must be so difficult.' Well, what am I going to say? I may say, 'Oh yes, it's very difficult,' when I don't really feel that way. There are real stresses; I don't mean to minimize that. But I think that the form of communication that goes on when women don't know each other very well tends to reinforce difficulties. The myth starts to take on its own reality. You feel you have to say certain things or risk being seen as incredibly audacious, or arrogant, or in denial."

- Not acknowledging the contribution you are making in caring for children. Since caring for children is unpaid, frequently invisible, and generally devalued by society, it's harder to ask for and accept needed help. You might view yourself as being "needy" for having children, which you are, but forget to view yourself as a hero for caring for your children and contributing to the future, which you also are.

◻ Fear that you can't reciprocate when you need help. You probably can't, but this situation is temporary. You may fear that people will think less of you or resent you because you can't reciprocate. They might.

◻ Fear of obligation or of becoming overextended emotionally.

◻ Mistrust of people who offer to help or agree to help. What if "helpers" are not being honest about their own limits and, because they can't say no, resent or avoid you? This fear often is well founded. People frequently overextend themselves, then resent the person whom they've helped, or they withdraw to protect themselves from their own inability to say no.

◻ Ignorance of how to create a support system. How do you find other parents at work who want to talk honestly about their lives and share resources? How do you get your workplace to help you connect with other parents? How do you develop a babysitting co-op? How do you create trust, guidelines, and open communication?

◻ Recognizing the real cost of social support. The time you spend investing in supportive relationships is time that you are not spending alone, or alone with children, or alone with your partner. The quality of support must be high to make the expenditure of time and energy worthwhile.

People who are able to create good support systems aren't necessarily free from these feelings, pressures, and limits. They just find ways to overcome them. They begin by making support a priority. Fortunately, we have many role models to help us learn to develop social support systems: immigrants and refugees whose cultures are more family centered and group focused, such as those from Asia, Latin America (especially Central America), and Africa; single parents, who create strong, reciprocal support systems out of sheer necessity; and, a group that often combines both categories, African-American women, who have been caring for each other's children and creating strong communities for many years.

Broadening Your Concept of What Can Be Shared

To begin developing a support system, enlarge your picture of what kinds of support are possible. Here are a few ways the parents we interviewed said they support each other.

Truthful Communication

Communicate truthfully about everything, especially what it's really like to live with children and work at a job. Help each other get the big picture to better appreciate the small picture of each moment. "I just try to be as available as I can to support my friends who are going to have kids," explains Lena, who recently cut back her work schedule as a consultant to spend more time with her 3-year-old son. "How can you prepare somebody for what's to come? There really isn't any literature or discussion about what kind of issues come up once you've had the child, where that fits in your life as a woman, as a wife, your new role as a mother, even in terms of being a daughter, or having a grandmother, two grandmothers. And then add work to that!"

Discover that you're not alone, that others are experiencing the same problems and feelings. Diana says, "My life is so busy, and it never calms down. I'm trying to get perspective. So I called a really good friend and I asked her, 'Am I trying to do too much, or is too much being asked of me and I'm responding appropriately?' "

Speaking honestly provides a welcome jolt of reality and helps provide a more accurate perspective on your choices and experiences. The guilty, envious working mother compares her situation to an idealized mother at home, not to the reality, and vice versa. Patricia observes, "If you get support in every phase of your life, then the work-family conflict is nowhere near as great. I still wake up in the middle of the night, and if I think about the number of hours in my child's life that I am 'missing,' it's more than I had dreamed of. And then I remember what I do all day on Saturday when the kids are around and I realize that happens when I'm at home too."

Enlarged Perspective

You may be happy today, but someone else is sad. Tomorrow, or soon, it will be your turn to be sad. We take turns. "There was always a sense of humor, always something to laugh about," Linda says about her network of parents. "If it wasn't your kid, you could see someone else's kid driving their parents nuts or going through some stage that your kid just went through. I think about having schlepped two baskets of laundry to the laundromat every Sunday with a kid for almost ten years. I don't know how I did it. But there was always Sandy running around taking taxis or buses with her kid to get anywhere, always someone having a more difficult time."

Listening

Listening is the most important thing people can do for each other most of the time. Listen to the joy and the pain. Don't insist that someone have a problem before you'll listen. Don't wait until you have a problem before asking someone to listen to you. And don't hesitate to listen, and to ask others to listen to you, when you do have a problem. Listening does not require that you solve the problem or even necessarily that you have any ideas.

When someone truly listens to you, you experience your situation from a larger perspective, even if the person doesn't say a single word. When you can talk honestly about your conflict, you can work it through and come to your own solution. The listening doesn't make it easy or make the pain go away, but it helps you to identify your own priorities, take responsibility for your own choices, and understand the parameters in which those choices occur.

Understanding and Appreciation

Parenting is hard work, which can feel invisible if nobody else is there to appreciate it. Parenting and working expand the challenges and, potentially, the rewards. We may regard ourselves as inadequate bumblers rather than the masters of balance, focus, and commitment that we are unless we help each other see these dimensions of ourselves. "When I found this community of friends, it was like a breath of fresh air," Linda says. "I wasn't being criticized for who I was or what I was trying to do. I found people who understood me."

Fun

One of the best parts of social support is sharing the fun of parenting and family life. Single and coupled parents in our group created more fun in their limited time away from work by sharing holiday celebrations, excursions, camping trips, and family vacations.

"We've started to plan family vacations," says Lena. "There are twenty-one people, and this past summer we caravaned up to Sacramento to the state fair and rented all these rooms and the kids played together. The group is going to go up to the snow country in January. My friend with twins and I meet at the public market once a month."

Child Care

Most people with good support systems have the attitude that their children are often enriched by the time they spend with other people. "Social support wasn't just child care, but that's how it started," recalls Alice:

> Initially, it was what I needed the most—somebody to take care of my son so I could get my one or two hours to myself, beyond work. From when he was 9 months old until he was 18 months old, two men friends took care of him six hours a day, three days a week, just for love. Then as he got older, we developed a whole system of social support that was somewhat friend based, peer based, and institutionally based through a child care center and then an elementary school.

"The close friend who'd been our childbirth teacher and ended up being my partner and coach at the birth would take care of my son," says Judith. "I bought her a car seat, and she was his mommy when I would go swimming or to therapy. People in our town would wonder who I was because they were so used to seeing her with him when she took him to swim class. She was his godmother and really was a support system for me."

Transportation

You have a crazy shift? Someone else doesn't. Ask for help. The carpool rituals, songs, jokes, and landmarks will create wonderful memory stories for your children in about fifteen years.

Food

Cook together on weekends, share meals, go shopping for each other, share use of a freezer so you can buy food in bulk. Have potluck dinners on a regular basis. Some workplaces offer nutritious meals from the company cafeteria that working parents (and other hurried people) can buy at low cost to heat and serve when they get home. Request that school meetings include dinner and child care for families. Or ask schools to provide dinner and child care, even without the meeting. "Sometimes at lunch time I would drop by the child care center and ask if this was the parent care center," remembers Alice. "They decided that it probably was. They fed me."

Community Resources: The Inside Story

Find out what services exist, which ones are truly useful, and how to access them. Examples of useful community organizations include family resource centers, parenting classes and support groups, child care resources and referral networks and switchboards, twenty-four-hour parenting crisis hot lines, advocacy organizations for children and families, family organizations run by churches and synagogues, and many others. Use, and encourage other parents to use, those resources. They're not just there for those "other needy" people. Contribute to them too if you can.

Advocacy

Support each other to confront institutions, such as schools, child care centers, colleges and universities, churches and synagogues, and workplaces, to ask for the changes that you need for your family. "We go with parents as allies," says Ethel Seiderman, director of Parent Services Project, Inc. "We're not ashamed to be identified as advocates for the family. If a parent is going for a parent-teacher conference, we'll say, 'Would you like us to go with you?' And we'll let the school know that we're coming together. And if the school's a little intimidated, maybe that's okay because it's been the other way for so long."

Help community institutions make it possible for you to contribute by asking them to provide varied opportunities for your input, and to schedule meetings, with child care, at times you can attend.

Shared Possessions and Services

Buy things in common; barter for goods or services. Someone knows how to cut hair, repair the furnace, fix the loose thread on the sweater, unravel the communication mishap, heal the sick tree in the yard. We don't all have to do everything, buy everything, know everything. That's why we have each other.

Life Passages

Birth, death, and lesser changes—a new job, the loss of a job, a transfer, a child's movement from one stage to another, an illness, an alteration in some important relationship—are times of great energy and often stress. At these transitions, you especially need to help each other and let others help you. "I hadn't expected my friend and childbirth coach to be in my bed the night of the birth, but my husband was out of town, and I went into labor during the labor rehearsal of our childbirth class. So we went home together and had a baby," says Judith.

Sources of Support

It is important to be flexible in seeking support and to create a diverse support system. Different people can provide varied perspectives and unique kinds of support: youngsters and oldsters, people with children and those without, men and women, people who work at jobs, people who care for family members, people who do both. Life is richer for this diversity.

Partners

For many, the support of their partner is a key factor in their happiness, regardless of how they divided their work and family roles. Wendy and Karl, parents of a 2-year-old son, both work full time. Karl explains the system they devised that offers each maximum support:

> We each have some time to ourselves now. If we want to schedule it in the evening, for example, we would take our son home and I would feed him, and Wendy would have about an hour to do whatever she wants. Then we would trade off, and Wendy would be with him, or he could play by himself for another hour. I go to sleep later than Wendy, so on weekends she gets up a little earlier with him, takes care of breakfast, and spends the first couple of hours with him so I can get up when I want. And then I'll take care of him, or we'll all play together. That's worked pretty well.

Wendy agrees: "Any way you cut it, I'm very fortunate. Karl does more than 50 percent."

Even some parents who were divorced, amicably or otherwise, received significant support from their child's other parent, which helped them to balance work and family. This kind of support was mentioned most frequently by people who shared joint custody. "I have to give Amy's dad some credit because he has been consistent with child support," says Linda. "Right now it's probably not a very generous amount, but the consistency has given me some breathing space. And I had breathers in the five years Amy was gone during the summer. It's a nightmare for some people to have to find child care in the summer."

Matt describes the good relationship he has with his ex-wife as instrumental in his ability to create balance. "The way we do it," he explains, "is that every Sunday and Monday nights my children are at my house, and Tuesdays, Wednesdays, and Thursdays they are at Gretchen's house. And then we alternate weekends. Gretchen travels periodically so weeks that she travels I pick up those days. We are pretty flexible. It comes out to about fifty-fifty, but we don't track it."

Relatives

Those lucky enough to have family close by could hardly imagine parenting and working without this resource. There were ethnic differences among our interviewees in the availability of extended family. Almost every Asian parent we interviewed, for example, relied intensely on extended family. This kind of support was generally less available for most of our interviewees of every other ethnic group.

Wendy describes with great enthusiasm her family support:

> The two grandmas are both very involved. Karl's mom lives in a neighboring county and comes to stay with us two and a half days a week. Usually Sunday nights Karl and I can go out to dinner alone. She also might stay at home with Sam on Monday. She brings food for him, food for us. On other days, my mother would love to babysit. For emergencies, if someone is sick, I call my mom, and she has never said no. She'll change her plans. She lives five blocks away. I just count my blessings every day. I love seeing Sam with his grandparents. I purposely go away and just look at them. I love the continuity.

Lisa and Ray also have their extended family on both sides close to them. Lisa says they never have to worry about who's going to take care of their son "because there is someone there to help all the time."

The presence, or lack, of this kind of support makes an unbelievable difference in parents' lives.

Friendship Networks

Many people whose relatives are not nearby create substitute extended families through friends. When Suzanna's baby was 6 months old, an acquaintance of hers had a baby: "We had initiated a little bit of contact, enough that we thought we would be able to have a friendship. We spent the next year together, every day, and

I think that is what saved me—having another woman to talk to. We became close friends at a time when my husband couldn't really be available a lot because he was traveling for his job."

Linda, a single parent, relied on the support of friendships with other parents and children. "What I think was helpful back then was our creating a network," she explains. "We had the kids in our life, and it was okay to take time off. None of us knew how we should do it. We would all get together to have our spaghetti dinners and the kids would all be playing in the living room and we would be talking. And we would shut the door. There was always someone who was deeply interested in your kid as much as you were. There was that kind of extended family." Almost fifteen years later, scattered throughout different communities, many of those parents and children still provide support to each other.

Employed Help

Judith was especially articulate about the depth of support she has received from people she has employed:

> In the first years of being a mother, I saw a therapist two times a week. Mostly she kept me company and was a good mother to me while I learned how to be a mother myself. Also, when my daughter was 4 months old, before I returned to work, a really splendid child care person came into our lives in the nick of time. She was pregnant at the time, but was far and away the best candidate. She came the three days a week I worked and took such good care of our house and such good care of the children that, in a very silent way, she taught me how to be a good homemaker. I'd never had laundry folded so carefully, never had a garden watered so perfectly, never had meals cooked so nicely. And, lo and behold, after she left, I was a better housekeeper. I was really touched by the experience of being taught, not being instructed, but being given to until finally I wanted to do things nicely myself.
>
> I've always chosen, at first unconsciously and now more consciously, people who were strong in the ways I wasn't. I'm sort of high energy and speedy and impatient

and passionate, and I've tended to hire calm, efficient, patient, serene people. The children have had a series of adults in their lives who've loved them, who've been really impressive role models, who've been antidotes to areas where their father and I were not particularly strong and who, without exception, are still important people in their lives. They come and visit us, write at holidays, and are members of our extended family.

Support at the Workplace

Some people we interviewed experienced significant support at work, through formal policies or through informal relationships. Wendy found that things worked out better than she ever imagined at her workplace:

> I didn't know when I came to the company that they were planning a child care center. I got to meet with the designer. I got very excited, though I was trying not to be, since they were letting people in only by lottery and I felt I had a slim chance. At first my son didn't get in, but then we got a spot from a wait list. Karl drops us off. I leave Sam, then come upstairs. Karl comes back, picks us up. I can go see Sam any time.

Patricia works at a large corporation, but when her children were small, she worked for a nonprofit agency that advocated for children and families. Her daughter went with Patricia to the workplace until she was a year old. Patricia says:

> I remember that first year or two of being a parent when it was just hell. I think at that point some kind of peer support can be very helpful. I couldn't find it except in my work environment. And that was just so lucky. The women at work were my mother and my grandmother. I haven't seen my real mother in twenty-two years. My husband and I have no relatives on the West Coast. And everybody I knew was just beginning to have babies. We were all stumbling around in the dark. They really helped me, like when one said, "Shara's pulling at her ear; she might have

an ear infection." Or, "It's really kind of hard to get these shoes on her feet. Patricia, your kid needs new shoes." Just those small things that in a different time I would have gotten from my relatives or neighbors across the backyard fence, I got there.

Community Organizations and Institutions

Community organizations, including schools and child care centers, can provide significant support. Judith joined a mother-baby group when her first child was born: "Those moms are still close friends. We get together about once a week at someone's house, and the boys—we all had boy babies—are still good friends thirteen years later. So that became our community. We found out what was normal and what wasn't. We gave each other feedback. We took care of each other's babies. All those things were great!"

Sharon found support through her church:

> My faith is not the sort of thing I wear on the outside. I just know it's there, and the religious experience gives my daughter and me a common bond. She really likes the church, for its social outlets and for the other things that are there. It's amazing. It gives us an even stronger level of communication about different things than we talked about before. That's really enjoyable to me, very precious. Although I don't think either one of us would be seen as a Bible-carrying religious person, I think we're both very spiritual. It keeps me from going crazy from time to time.

Parent Services Project, Inc. (PSP) is a national organization that helps child care centers, early education sites, and schools provide support to parents and other family members. The program started with four child care centers and graduated to eight within two years and now has spread to 300 early childhood sites and 15,000 families in six states. The parents, in partnership with staff, create a menu of services to be provided to families on a regular basis. Director Ethel Seiderman pointed out that parents "don't need support the third Tuesday of every month. You need it there so you can plug into it on a regular basis. Support would be the staff member or the director who's available just to rap. Support would be the picnic we did yesterday where you just gather and there's no intention that you're going to divulge your innermost secrets." PSP child care centers offer respite child care; parents can leave their children with their friends and teachers at night at the center while the parents go out and have fun doing anything they want, and the children regard the occasion as a huge treat. PSP also offers parent groups, parent classes, social excursions for parents, family field trips, and workshops on a broad range of topics, all chosen by parents.

Neighborhoods

A few interviewees described the support they received within their immediate communities. "We have a great neighborhood," says Lena, who lives in a suburban town. "The houses were new when we bought them, so we created our neighborhood. The kids pour out of the houses, and the mothers are all standing there watching and we talk to each other. I feel lucky because it's not like that in a lot of neighborhoods."

Alice, who lives in the middle of a city, was also lucky enough to live in a family-friendly neighborhood:

> When my son was in elementary school, we lived in a two-story flat, and both of the people who lived downstairs had grown up on the block. Her parents lived across the street, and his parents lived down the street. They had two children, who were cared for by her parents while they both worked. The father had three brothers and a sister who all lived within a block. They would cruise by and check on them. Like other city neighborhoods, most of the people on the block didn't know each other, but just this much support was enough to draw all the children out of their houses. There were hordes of them who played together outside all the time after school and on weekends, even though they all went to different schools and were of many different races and cultures. It's amazing that such a small thing could make such a huge difference. My son went into shock when he was 11, and we moved to a different neighborhood where there were no

children on the streets. When all of his social life had to be planned and involved transportation, it was not the same at all.

Many more of our parents remember such support from their childhoods and lament its lack in their lives now. A few people had begun to organize change within their neighborhoods. Craig says, "In our neighborhood, as an extension of the family, we have a babysitting co-op, and somebody organized a neighborhood watch, looking out for your fellows on the block. That just started a week ago. It seems like people are saying, 'I can't rely on institutions to deal with this. I have to do it.' And I think that's exciting."

Others in a Similar Situation

A particular kind of support comes from peers: other single parents, full-time employed mothers, parents of twins, fathers taking a significant role in caring for their children, parents of a child with a disability, people who are caring for their aging parents. Such support gives you someone who understands the context of your experience and with whom a more reciprocal relationship is possible.

Sometimes peer support occurs relatively spontaneously. "The agency I work in is predominantly women of color," says Isabel. "It's really great because we all understand the common struggle that we have in terms of having to work, and where we've come from historically. A lot of us have similar things in our families and in our communities that we can relate to—for example, having to struggle to go to school and not having the money to do it or being the only ones in our families with educations."

As a working mother, Kate needs support from peers:

At Claire's school, I don't know if it's like the caste system or what, but I know the mothers who work. We're the ones who always show up at the end of the day together and we talk, and then Claire gets to know these children. The girls make the connection because they're in the after-care program together. There's this kind of quasi community of the working moms, and then there is everybody else. It happens that we find each other.

In other instances, peer support is created by organized support groups of people who share a common experience. These groups are convenient for working parents if they meet at work—for example, during the lunch hour. Sometimes such groups are sponsored by community organizations. For many working parents, attending such groups is impossible unless they offer child care, provide food or opportunities for parents to bring food, and are scheduled in the evening or on weekends. They also work well at schools or child care centers, if child care is provided in a setting where the children already feel comfortable.

These efforts are creating a burgeoning sense of community. For some parents, this experience is new; for others, it's the re-creation of the community support they experienced as children.

Sharon says that the black community has always emphasized effective, informal support:

> There's always been a sense that people did what needed to be done with less emphasis on roles as such. If you were around to do it, then you took care of the kids, whether you were a neighbor or a sister or a mother. Somebody was always there. That kind of support is not present in the same way, at least not in my experience. But I think people are trying to develop that. In some ways it's similar to the relationship I've had with some of my women friends; the difference is that all of us are without extended family and without the fathers of the children. It means a different kind of availability.

Craig and his wife are considering bringing his mother to live with them, a change that started his thinking about family and community life: "It suddenly struck me that it's almost like going back. People tried this separateness for a while, in their own little compact units, and found that really unfulfilling. I think I'm going back to this vision of a bigger unit, a bigger support system, that starts with me and my family and then it goes to the community and beyond."

Skills That Help Create Supportive Relationships

There are specific skills that are helpful in creating a support system. In a society that does not emphasize mutuality or cooperation, many people are not taught these fundamentals.

Recognizing Your Isolation

Acknowledge the consequences of your isolation, and your beliefs and attitudes that might be perpetuating it. Your own isolation can be invisible because it seems so normal if you've never experienced anything different and if the people around you act as if it is normal to live this way.

Taking Responsibility for Being a Person With Needs

If you've always been self-reliant, you may not understand why you're having such a hard time now that you're trying to work and care for children, and you may blame yourself or the people around you (partner, children, family, friends, coworkers). When you acknowledge your isolation, you can take steps to create change. There will be times when you have to be alone and when no one else can help. But it's also essential, for you and for your children, to find the support you need. Your children gain from having less stressed parents, and they learn that people are social beings who need and can rely on each other.

Cultivating a Positive Approach

Working is good, and parenting is good. You want to share your child and your life, not your burden. Creating a network of mutual support will benefit society as a whole directly, through the healthy children who develop in your family, and indirectly, through the supportive, child-positive, family-friendly community that will grow in part through your efforts. That we need each other is a fact of human existence. We can support each other in ways that enhance our lives and respect our individual needs and differences.

Enlarging Your Definition of Reciprocity

When you're caring for dependent children or aging parents, the people in your care cannot reciprocate. Children may be able to do so later in life, and elderly parents have cared for others earlier in their lives. But now it's their turn to be cared for and your turn to do the caring. Being the caretaker means that you usually cannot be in equal, reciprocal relationships with other people who are not also caring for dependents. You're very much on the giving side of the equation overall, though you may be temporarily on the taking side with other adults. The ledger can only be balanced over time, and not necessarily with the same individuals who provided you with support. "My mother always taught us that it all comes from the same place and it all goes to the same place," observes Alice.

Asking for Help and Appreciating Yourself for Reaching Out

People may have different degrees of need for help, but most share an aversion to asking. In this self-sufficiency–revering culture, needing and asking for help can make you feel demeaned. To avoid this feeling, many people maintain a facade of being in control and never ask for anything. Others are unable to accept genuine offers of help, even when they're really in need.

Judith, who works 75 percent time, remembers how impossible it was for her to ask for help after her second child was born:

> Ben, who was 2½ at the time, had lost his mom, but I didn't know it, and this witch had come to live in her place. I'd like to have those six months expunged from the record. I had lost my child care person who also was my friend. My son was this monster in my face. I look at the pictures of him then, this tiny child still in diapers crawling in his baby sister's basket with his bottle, and I realize I had two babies and could have used a great deal more support. My husband was working and studying between sixty and seventy hours a week by choice. I believe I felt very abandoned. In my mothers' group, every one of them eventually had second children spaced five years apart, so

they were watching with horror and fascination to see what would happen to me. I remember thinking, "I'm going to beat this child if I don't get them to sleep at the same time." I complained to my friends, and they would sympathize, but when I look back now, I think I needed to say to them, "I need to come to someone's house every day at 2:00 P.M. and sleep for an hour while you watch your baby and mine," and I didn't know how to ask. Okay, so live and learn.

Asking Early, Before You're in a Total Crisis

Many people are happy to help with small things, but few people are able to take over your life when you are falling apart. Unfortunately, many people wait until that point before asking for help.

When Alice's son was a toddler, they lived in a city where she knew few people:

> The people next door to me had two girls, just a little older than he was. I wasn't close to them, and we shared few interests, but I made it a point to get to know them. Their house had two stories, which was a revelation: The children could actually play upstairs, and we could sit and talk. We could hear them, they knew we were nearby, but they weren't right in our faces. As a single parent, this was an experience I craved. Several times, as I was starting to lose my mind, I called these neighbors and asked if they would be willing to watch James for fifteen minutes. I know they thought I was completely mad, but they never said no. In fifteen minutes I could take a shower, I could cry, I could read one section of the newspaper, I could stare out the window at a tree. I'm convinced those fifteen minutes saved both of our lives several times.

Recognizing the Value of Helping to the Helper

If needing help too often feels awful, helping usually feels great. Allowing people who truly are in a position to help us to do so is a gracious gift. They are not trying to balance work and family in the same way we are, are not parents of small children, are not single parents, and they have more time, energy, and resources than we do. Many people would like opportunities to be involved with children. Others who don't understand the issues of balancing work and family would like to learn. Still others would like to help but have no idea how to connect. If people ask if there is anything they can do to help, say yes. It doesn't matter if you can't think of anything you need right now. You will. Get their telephone number, and call them when you need help.

Letting People Help in Ways That Make Them Happy

Find out who likes to take care of children, cook meals, make phone calls, provide information and resources, who knows how to negotiate with a boss or communicate with an angry partner, who has a car and would be happy to drive, who has a child at home who needs company. Find people who not only can help but for whom helping enhances their lives. Believe that this kind of matching is possible, and then look for it and ask for it.

"My mother, who didn't like being a mother, loves being a grandmother," observes Jean. "She nurtures the creative part of my son. She won't make any regular commitments, but she will come stay with him when he's sick. They have a great time together, and she doesn't have to share him with anyone else."

Being Honest About the Specificity of Your Need for Support

Too many of our conversations revolve around giving and fending off each other's suggestions or helpful gestures when they aren't appropriate. Advice is a waste of everyone's time if we aren't interested in it. Someone to care for our child is not helpful if what we really want is help with something else so we can spend time with the child.

Identify what you need, and ask for that specifically. While flexibility is good up to a point—maybe you need something that you haven't thought of yet—say no to help that doesn't fit your needs or your timing. Pretending to accept unhelpful help wastes everyone's time and inevitably leads to hurt feelings.

It seems very ungracious to say, "Excuse me but that advice doesn't really fit what I need right now. I just want you to listen to me." But truthfulness is really in everyone's interest, especially if you convey that you are as concerned about the giver's time as you are about your own. Changing these practices is hard to do alone, and much easier in a community of people who are all working together to create a climate of mutual respect and trust.

Reaching Out to Help Others

Many people trying to balance work and family feel so overwhelmed that they can't imagine how they can be helpful to anyone else. But there are countless ways that you can help now, and even more ways you will contribute later when your life evens out a little bit. If you have extra time, find people who are trying to balance work and family, especially single parents, and offer to help them. Don't give any advice or suggestions without the other person's specific permission. Sometimes it helps to offer specific help; a person not used to getting help might not be able to imagine what she wants. Be persistent and patient if the person says no the first time. Tell the person why you want to help—what's in it for you. Remind the person that you too have needed help in the past and will need help in the future, that it was hard for you to ask and accept, and that the energy exchanges will even out in time. Make sure it does even out by being vulnerable and asking for help for yourself from that person or from someone else. Work to balance these roles in your own life.

Refraining From Overextending Yourself

"I've definitely slowed down since I had the baby," says Janice. "I'm no longer pretending to do everything all at once. I'm not unavailable to people, but I'm not as available as I used to be. When someone contacts me or needs me, I don't feel like I have to do it for them or save them like I did before because I don't have the time or the energy. And I'm much more likely to sit back, listen, reflect, and give support."

Selecting Institutions That Foster Social Support

It's a good idea to select schools or child care centers not just because of their academics, computers, facilities, and grounds but by the extent to which they support working parents and facilitate their relationships with each other. All community institutions—schools, churches, libraries, recreation centers, parks, and the workplace itself—can help people meet and support each other by providing a warm and welcoming atmosphere, opportunities to get to know each other, child care, food, transportation, and an environment that supports diversity, as well as schedules and policies that help working parents.

Lena's son's child care center is a place with a newsletter for parents, parent participation on committees, Saturday clean-ups, monthly parent meetings, and events. "Part of it is to give us ownership of the center," she says. "I used to be on the board, which slowly became a parent board and then a community board. Finding that kind of quality child care is a real key."

Alice found her son's elementary school "completely lovely and very supportive and focused on relationships, for the children and for the parents. It had after-school care with people who loved the children and cared about them. And his friends today are the friends he knew from that school."

Creating What You Need

If you are in an isolated situation, it's important to create support at home, at work, and in your community, formally or informally. It can begin with an individual effort and is strengthened by working cooperatively with other people.

"When I first moved to San Francisco, my son was 9 months old," says Alice:

> I didn't know anyone else with children his age. I was walking down the street, carrying him, when I noticed some mothers with toddlers. I introduced us, we started talking, and within ten minutes I asked them if they were interested in exchanging child care. They looked at me as though I were insane. But a few weeks later, when one of them discovered a new day care center that was opening

nearby, she called me and I was able to get him on the waiting list for when he turned 2. It took a little while longer before we were exchanging child care. We wouldn't have made it without each other. It was worth their thinking I was crazy.

Leah Fisher at The Center for Work and the Family describes how she organized a new parent support organization called Birthways. "Birthways was what I did to have a group of friends and a support network to educate myself [during pregnancy]. I was very grateful to have it."

How Social Support Needs Change Over Time

One of the most surprising things about having children is that relationships often change completely. Since we're utterly transformed by the birth of our children, we might expect accompanying changes, but the magnitude of the alteration of relationships often catches us off-guard. On the simplest level, we tend to spend more time with people with children, regardless of whom we spent time with before. As the children grow and change, our networks change as well, a potentially disorienting experience. Just as we think we have finally organized support, the children change schools, or want to pick their own friends, or are no longer satisfied with after-school care, or otherwise move on to something new, suddenly plunging us into renewed disequilibrium.

Relationships can also transform when our lives change in other ways. We leave a job, return to a job, go back to school. We become more or less focused on the parenting dimension of our lives. We get divorced or get married. Suddenly we have to start all over to create our systems of social support. All this change is less stressful if we anticipate it and if we remember that nothing that we build lasts forever.

It's crucial not to feel inadequate because we don't have support or if we can't easily overcome our isolation. A social problem of this magnitude is not going to change overnight by individual efforts alone. It's not realistic to believe that we can overcome all of our fears and insecurities about mutual support just by reading a book or deciding to change. And it's not realistic to believe that we can single-handedly create community in such an individualistic society. This process of finding support is a collective as well as an individual challenge. We need to appreciate ourselves and each other for every step we take along the way and to talk to each other openly about how we are working on this issue. Our reward will be a better life for ourselves and our children.

Every time we ask for help or allow someone else to help us, we're participating in the creation of a better society. According to Ethel Seiderman of Parent Services Project, Inc., "We're reshaping the paradigm in this country, away from saying you have to close off what your weaknesses are and not ask for help. What I say is, the minute you let somebody know you need help you're on the way to getting it. That's a strength, not a weakness."

10

Integration

On the idyllic level, I wanted to belong to a place where work and family and life were just all one thing. It wasn't something that you went away to do. You didn't choose between your kids and your community.

—Karin, a nurse, married, and mother of a son,
age 15, and a daughter, age 11

We are more than our work identities and our family identities. Although the parents we interviewed gave us innumerable practical reasons for wanting to balance work and family, many said they were seeking something beyond balance, which they described as a sense of unity. They sought to deepen their relationship to work, to family, to themselves, and to the world. We call this quest for something beyond balance "integration."

"I have a friend who's a new mother, and I recently asked her how she was doing," says Judith David. "She told me, 'My job is great; I love it, and I'm doing well in it. I love my daughter. I'm having a lot of fun with her, and we've got our child care arrangements in place. It's all working. All the pieces of my life are fine. It's just feeling that they don't all tie together that's the problem.' "

Even the terminology to describe the need to integrate the parts of our lives is insufficient, says David:

> Before it was child care, and then it was work and family, and now it's kind of work and life. But then there's a work part of life. I don't even like the term "balancing" that much. "Juggling" I definitely don't like because it seems

out of control, unstable. Juggling is something you do for a little while, then things fall apart, and you have to pick up everything again. And balancing—just off the top of my head, it makes me think there are distinct, separate entities, and one gets more weight and one gets less. I don't think that the entities are that separate. There's a lot of overlap and crossover. It just seems more integrated, more interwoven.

Whose Children?

What we are calling "integrating work and family" is not a fully developed concept, but we can identify some of the elements that point in its direction. Primary among these is a greater connection between the world of work and the world of children and family. As long as children are viewed as the private, individual responsibility of their parents and are expected to be kept separate from the overall life of the community, balance between work and family is the highest goal that parents are likely to be able to achieve. If children were regarded as being, in part, the responsibility, and future, of everyone, and if society included them as fully participating human members, work and family issues would transform.

On a societal level, the quest for integration relates to the need to heal a number of splits: between men and women, childhood and adulthood, production and leisure, working mothers and stay-at-home mothers, efficiency and caring, and public and private spheres of responsibility. One factor that perpetuates the split between the world of children and caretaking and that of work is the relatively brief historical moment when many mothers stayed home and cared for children while fathers worked for money away from the home. Now that most mothers are in the workforce and more fathers than previously are caring actively for their children, this extreme chasm between work and family is increasingly dysfunctional.

A model of integration is part of the psychological theory of the great psychoanalyst Erik Erikson, who identified "generativity" as one of the critical stages of healthy adult development: For adults to develop their full potential, they need at some point to give back to the next generation. This giving could be accomplished through parenting, through giving to actual children, or giving to any aspect of life that would benefit future generations.[1] People are helped to express their generativity when the world of work incorporates the concerns of parents and families and when the community incorporates the needs of children and the people who care for them. Generativity is also enhanced when people who are not parents become involved with children and more generally with the betterment of their communities.

It is helpful to keep in mind the context of generativity, and how far we are from a society that integrates children into the mainstream of life, when we consider parents' strategies to integrate their work and family identities.

Isolation vs. Integration

The culture of the United States rewards self-sufficiency, autonomy, privacy, stoicism, mobility, and individualism. These values are extremely important, but they are also limited. Humans are social animals, dependent on one another and interconnected, and the culture too often dismisses this aspect of our nature. The result is that many of us find it hard to accept our need for others and strive for a kind of isolating self-sufficiency that is humanly impossible.

For many people, the kind of isolation that has become "normal" in this culture becomes intolerable when they have children. The culture idealizes an image of a lone mother and child, or children, interacting intensely during the day until a lone father returns from work. In fact, this picture is increasingly rare, and, in many cases, it is unsatisfying for the participants. Unfortunately, the reality that has replaced the ideal is often also isolated and stressed: a single parent or couple who work all day and then race to pick up their children to be alone with them all night, exhausted and pressured. Working parents frequently lack flexible, interconnected alternatives.

According to Jeree Pawl,

> There's no more center square, no communal village life.
> Today there's a loss of the sense of family and of commu-

nity. People seek work and companionship, but it's all in a weird context—a context of isolation. People are lonely. An older couple I know having their first child live in a neighborhood where nobody is home from morning to night. It's like a deserted island. It is not fun for the mother to stay home in these conditions, so she'll work, they'll get a live-in au pair, and the child will have no sense of living anywhere except in a box. Taking care of children in isolation is a very odd thing to do. In the past you would have done it in the context of community.

Isolation can be physical, and it also can be emotional. When Julie returned to work when her son was 6 weeks old, she was surrounded by people who had no idea of how her life and heart had been transformed with the birth of her son. She reflects on her time at home: "I was alone with a baby who couldn't communicate. It was just the baby and me, and no one else. It struck me as so odd going from being with adults all the time to having to make a plan to talk to someone. It seemed unnatural. At work you can feel isolated, and at home you can too."

Parents' isolation can be exacerbated by their efforts to combine work and family. Often they lack any discretionary time and feel constrained from participating in parent groups or other activities that could lead to friendship networks with other parents. The physical and emotional distance between work and home can create a gulf, making it difficult to develop integrated relationships in either place. To the extent that the workplace separates itself from its employees' family concerns, parents may not feel safe talking to coworkers about their lives as parents. They may have well-founded fears that discussing family issues will get them labeled as uncommitted to work, weak, or lacking appropriate boundaries.

The isolation in which parenting occurs is so extreme that the whole idea of a supportive community that could enhance parents' ability to work and care for their children is something many people can hardly imagine. "I would never dream of having society give me support," says Catherine. "I see our society as becoming quite fragmented. Despite the fact that I went to a government-run day care center, I'm not sure that there's much role for government in this. I don't know what we have left of community any more in this society, but we do have friendships. I think it's very important to have the support of good friends. But I just don't quite get the picture of how you would get support from society or from the community."

Karin stayed at home to care for her children, now ages 15 and 11, when they were little. She has a strong vision of parenting very young children with community support, although the reality she experienced was quite different:

> It makes me feel like crying when I remember it. I remember thinking, "God, I don't know anyone who's home. Everybody is out doing their life." Being home alone with an infant in that context was painful. I felt like I lost my identity. I felt like I didn't have any work. What I would have liked—the picture that comes into my mind—is bringing my kid down to the river to pound clothes on the rocks with other people and their kids. I wanted to be in a hunter-gatherer society—but without the drawbacks of my kid's getting sick and no medicine and women dying in childbirth.

Jeree Pawl noted, "When community collapses, we need to re-create it. There is a little park for children and families near where I live where parents and children gather. They have deliberately created a pocket of community in a very isolated world."

Searching Our Past for Role Models

In seeking role models it is helpful to attend to the complexities of our past, personal and social. There is often a tendency to oversimplify the past, to assume that there are no threads connecting our lives to those of previous generations.

Those of us who were raised by stay-at-home mothers and are raising our own children very differently may experience a sense of discontinuity with our past. Yet there have always been "working mothers," fully participating fathers, single parents, and various forms of mutual support among us. We need to find out more about how people in various cultures handle work and family, and talk to our friends and their children about what it feels like to live in varied families and communities.

It might be helpful to remember how unusual it is for parents and children to be isolated alone at home and how equally unusual it is for parents and children to spend their days in utterly separate realms. We might imagine what life would be like in a society that regularly provided extensive paid family leave for both parents and fully expected both mothers and fathers to make use of it. We need to explore the myriad ways that diverse people are re-creating some of these flexible, connected family forms, with friends, relatives, and members of their communities. As we join into this collective work, we can feel our rich connections to the histories of people all over the world.

Expressing Different Identities Simultaneously

Work-family advocates often suggest that working parents separate the spheres of work and family as a survival strategy, an approach that is effective for some parents. "I put in a ten- or twelve-hour day," says Patricia, "but when it's done, it's done. It's done emotionally and psychologically, and it's not even in my body any more. I can get rid of it."

Others, or the same people at different times, adopt an opposite strategy: They bring the skills, identities, and awareness of family into work and of work into family. Judith recalls an integrating moment when her son was about 2 weeks old and she was asked to speak at a conference. "Anna, who is his godmother and the childbirth teacher who came into our family at that point, sat in the audience and held Ben while I gave my twenty-minute presentation and then I went back into the audience and nursed him. I just remember the pleasure and the excitement of bringing these together—showing my baby to my work and having my baby with me at my work."

Wendy expresses this need for unity very explicitly. "I tried creatively bringing him to work," she says. "It didn't work, but it was fun, a joy. I did it one late afternoon and a couple of Saturdays. I liked seeing him in the office, blending these two parts of my life. I was so dedicated to my job that I spent most of my waking hours there. It was like bringing both sides of my life together. I wish I had a picture of him from that day sitting in my file cabinet in the office. I'd hang it up at home and at work."

Wendy also describes the satisfaction she received from such a simple thing as being able to talk openly about her child and family at work: "It's very freeing. At one point I worked with a team of engineering and construction employees. For nine months, we would see each other for half a day every month. We all have kids, and we'd all talk about them. After nine months we finally got out our pictures. Some of these guys had 30-year-old kids. People would say, 'Wait until your kid starts hating you.' I wanted to hear about that part too."

Children in the Workplace

More people than we ever expected talked about the benefits of bringing their children to work. Their experiences range from bringing the children occasionally in the evenings or the weekends when no one else was around, to bringing the children to work in an emergency, to working at places with on-site or nearby child care facilities, to making innovative arrangements to care for their children at work regularly. Yet this dimension of balancing—and integrating—work and family has received scant attention. After an initial push for on-site child care in the 1980s, this approach has been largely abandoned as too expensive and inefficient. And the fact that parents bring their children to work has been a secret that is rarely discussed openly. In other cultures, bringing children to work is a common practice.

Polly occasionally brings her 2-year-old to her office. "My daughter has been coming to the lab since she was 10 days old," she says. "It's neat to have her know what I'm doing at work, being exposed to a career in science. She has experienced it first-hand from early on. She'll have that to think about later. She went to lab meetings. It was great for my convenience and ease, everybody got to know her, and she got to know and be comfortable around many people."

Andrea, a single mother, is a co-owner of a family business, a conservative commercial real estate office. During her pregnancy she arranged for the firm to hire a person who would work half-time as a bookkeeper and half-time, at her expense, as a child care provider for her child. The area they set up in the office eventually grew to resemble a miniature nursery school. When her child was an infant, she alternated caring for the child with the child care worker, slightly reducing her own work hours. She is now back to working full time, and her child, now 3½ years old, spends half-days at a child care center and half-days at the office, or in nearby parks, playgrounds, or organized activities, transported by her child care worker. Andrea is always nearby to oversee her care.

Janice also hired someone who worked in her office part time and cared for the baby part time:

> She's someone I have a close professional relationship with, and I know that I can trust her. The fact that the baby is just down the hall makes me feel great. We have a policy that I instituted at the office long before I got pregnant: If you have an older child or a toddler, with prior notice you can bring your child in for a limited number of hours if there's an emergency. That policy has turned around and allowed me to bring my baby in. The agreement is that there will be no children here on Tuesdays when most of the heavy interaction in the office and the staff meetings take place. It's worked really well. The office is used to having children around.

Kate's place of employment provides on-site child care. She doesn't use it herself, but a number of the people she supervises do:

> One of the people who works for me has a project that has both of us basically shut in a room working on this thing most of the day, but twice a day he goes down and gives Molly her medicine. He's gone for ten minutes; then he comes back. If he needs to stay late, he goes down there and brings Molly up, and she hangs out. We have toys in our office. Because I manage the group, I welcome it when people bring their children into work. I bring my kids into work occasionally.

As co-owners of a business or head of their work units, Andrea, Janice, and Kate had the power to create family-friendly policies. Elena dreams longingly about the luxury of having child care on site:

> That would be perfect. I think it would increase employee productivity, and also we could concentrate better on our jobs because we would know that our children are close by. I carpool to work with someone who works at a utility company, and she says that their child care center has been one of the best things the company has done for its employees. She says she even looks forward to coming to work in the mornings because she knows that her child is nearby. Every time she feels like checking on her child, she just goes and does it.

Bringing children to work has numerous advantages for parents and children. Parents spend more time with their children. They can provide hands-on care during the day, eat lunch together, share a special activity. The child gets access to the parent, learns about the world of work, and develops relationships with the parent's colleagues.

Marty has occasionally been able to include his daughters in his work projects:

> Sometimes they do a little bit of work with me. When my younger daughter was 9 or 10, she came in and did some data entry for me and stuffed envelopes. She did all the graphics on a computer program when she was only 10. My older daughter helped hand out questionnaires for a program evaluation we did. They can make extra money and be here with me. They get work experience, learn something new, and become more resourceful and independent. They're very computer literate and keep learning things. By the time they're older, they'll be very skilled and set for college and work.

Kate also felt that her children benefited by spending time at her workplace. She thinks "coming to work solves the mystery of where Mommy spends the day. When Claire goes to my work, she sees a picture of her and her artwork in the office. There is a part of her there. And the other thing is that they get to see their parent in a whole different environment—one that's not 'Put your socks on' and 'Can't you tie your own shoes?'—one that includes other adults."

Parents who don't work outside the home achieve the same benefits for their children by including them in the life of the community. "I combine my children's lives with the things I think are neat or important that I'm involved in," says Laura, a full-time mother of three who is also a writer. "They all come to my meetings when I'm working on a fundraiser and sort of participate. I get them interested in my life, and they're always intrigued. You show them your world. Kids love that, and it also helps me."

Several of the parents interviewed felt that the workplace benefits from the presence of children. It not only humanizes the situation; it also reminds people of the larger purpose of work: not just to make money or produce something but to benefit people. Janice felt that staff members' children's presence has a positive influence in her office:

> Since we do a lot of work with parents, it has helped some of the staff who don't have children. I think having children in the office contributes to the morale of the office because children always bring a smile. It's gotten everybody more cheerful, and considering the fact that we are being reorganized for the hundredth time and we've lost our director, morale here is positive and I think that it's because of the baby's presence. It just gives everyone a different perspective. Life goes on, you know, whatever happens. Her being here has slowed us down a little in a very positive way.

Part of transforming work along these lines seems to be reexamining the concepts of efficiency and speed and the relationship between productivity and nurturing. It's possible that we can accomplish what we need to with less racing, more caring, and more attention to why we are doing the work in the first place.

Working at Home

Another way to integrate the demands of work and family is working at home. This strategy lets parents be close to their children and lets children see what their parents do besides care for them. One problem is that it can be isolating. Still, many people value the chance to have all spheres of their lives under one roof.

Fred and his wife, Elizabeth, work at home whenever they can; this flexibility is a crucial factor in their efforts to create family balance and sanity. "Because of the kinds of jobs we have, we can work on a computer anywhere," he says. "That is a big relief and takes some of the pressure off. I'd like to do more of that. I miss some of the casual contact at work, which does have value. But an occasional day is not the end of the world. I can sit in my office and stare at a computer screen all day and not talk to anyone, or do it at home. Being at home helps with the pressure of the mornings and the afternoons."

Alice worked at home during most of her son's childhood, a fact that she said made it possible to be a single parent and

> not go totally crazy and not feel completely compromised as a parent. I could be with him when he was sick, when he needed a ride, when he forgot something, when he had homework, when he came home starving and disorganized. Of course, there's a downside. When he leaves home, I'll have years to heal from the stress of being interrupted so frequently for eighteen years. But it was totally worth it. I was able to support us, and I got to be an active, involved, available parent. Both were essential. I'll always be grateful for that, one of the greatest gifts.

Spending Time at Children's Schools

For children, the equivalent of integrating work and family is having parents or other family members come to their school or child care center. More than just the pleasure of being together, bringing adults into the world of children breaks down the artificial gap that exists in this culture between children and adults. Some

enlightened workplaces provide opportunities for their employees, parents and nonparents, to take time off to volunteer at
schools or youth service organizations, and allow parents to take
personal time off to participate in activities at their children's
school. Some educational programs arrange to have children visit
their parents' workplaces or bring parents, or other adults, to the
school to talk about work.

"When your parents are not at school and other parents are,
the child feels left out. It's very tough. I've been just continually
overwhelmed by how much it means to Josh when we go to
school, when we drive on field trips, when we do anything," says
Elizabeth of her 10-year-old son. "He's now this big fourth grader,
and if Fred or I show up in the classroom, he lights up. He left his
seat at his desk and came over and sat in his father's lap in his
classroom—total baby-like behavior. It just means so much to him
to have us there."

Kate's children went to a child care center that specialized in
the needs of working families. "That's another thing their school
does," she says. "They encourage you, if you can, to set up a tour
of your office for all the kids in the class. I've never done it because
I have trouble explaining to most adults what I do. But one mother
was the head of the youth hostel association. They went to the
youth hostel office and looked at the maps."

Wholeness

"Something that in the last maybe three or four years has really
helped me has been the recognition that some sort of spiritual
teaching was important to me," Sharon reflects. "Being a professional with at least three different roles in that alone—being a
mother, being a friend, being a lover from time to time—I have
so many hats that I wear, and my spiritual beliefs sort of keep me
from fragmenting. That is a very strong part of it. It's not just
that I'm less fragmented, but I'm more centered than I used to
be."

It is essential to have a vision that is integrated, connected,
and includes all of us. Can we see that we are actually linked to
each other? Can we experience that what really is needed is for
each of us to be exactly who we are, to make our own unique con-

tribution? Can we support each other to do so? Maybe there really is enough to go around: enough time, enough resources, enough love to care for each other and to care for our children, to support ourselves, and to do work that nourishes and improves the world.

Balancing work and family, and creating a life that reflects such a vision, is a work in progress. There are days when most of us look around and realize that we are overwhelmed, unbalanced, and exhausted once again. It is easy to get discouraged on those days. Part of creating balanced, integrated lives is to keep going, to forgive ourselves, to turn to our sources of support, internal and external, and to know that the effort itself is worthwhile.

Note

1. E. H. Erikson, *Childhood and Society,* 2d ed. (New York: W. W. Norton, 1963), pp. 266–268.

Wish List
Structural Changes for Creating Work-Family Balance

1. Provide tax breaks to companies that institute family-friendly policies and successfully incorporate these policies in practice. Distinguish between those companies that really apply these policies, according to their employees, and those for which family-friendly policies are more window dressing than reality.

2. Create a legitimized "family track," in which parents, or other people caring for dependents, temporarily reduce their work responsibilities; provide the option to return, without penalty, to a career track when their family responsibilities lessen.

3. Expand and extend opportunities for flexible and reduced hours to jobs that require high levels of competence and responsibility. Don't equate reduced time with reduced commitment, effectiveness, or responsibility. Provide opportunities for advancement for people who are working reduced or flexible hours.

4. Provide benefits for part-time work.

5. Create pay equity for men and women, so parents can choose whether one or both stay home to care for children based on family considerations.

6. Expand opportunities for parents to work at home and for children to come to work, all or part of the time. Consider providing on-site child care.

7. Encourage employees of both genders to make full use of the family leave policy that allows them to take unpaid time off to care for their newborn or newly adopted children.

8. Give people discretionary time off, to use for whatever they want. Let people take time off to care for their sick, or well, children, or for their sick, or well, selves.

9. Provide opportunities for employees to take paid time off work to do volunteer work, especially volunteer work that supports children and youth. Such a policy would let parents spend time in their children's child care programs or schools and would encourage other employees to contribute to the next generation.

10. Train middle managers on how to implement family-friendly policies.

11. Create a culture that reflects flexibility throughout the company and its systems.

12. Consider layoffs only as a last resort.

13. Seek a balance between the needs of the organization and the needs of the employees.

14. Schedule a retreat for employees. Go away somewhere. Put absolutely nothing on the agenda. Let people do whatever they want.

15. Provide opportunities for employees to communicate about and support each other regarding family responsibilities—for example, bulletin boards, newsletters, discussion groups, and workshops with opportunities for active participation.

16. Provide affordable health insurance that is separate from employment.

17. Conduct research to learn more about the perceptions of children about the impact of the workplace on family life.

18. Turn schools and child care centers into family care centers.

19. Focus media attention on couples who successfully share family and work responsibilities. Organize conferences and other forums that highlight successful balancing strategies.

20. Extend the school year.

Selected Readings

Aldous, J. (ed.). *Two Paychecks: Life in Dual-Earner Families*. Beverly Hills, Calif.: Sage, 1982.

Apter, T. *Working Women Don't Have Wives: Professional Success in the 1990's*. New York: St. Martin's Press, 1993.

Barnett, R. C., and Rivers, C. "The Myth of the Miserable Working Woman." *Working Woman* (February 1992): 62–65, 85–88.

Baruch, G. K., and Barnett, R. C. "Role Quality, Multiple Role Involvement, and Psychological Well-Being in Midlife Women." *Journal of Personality and Social Psychology* 51 (1986): 578–585.

Baruch, G., Barnett, R., and Rivers, C. *Lifeprints: New Patterns of Love and Work for Today's Woman*. New York: McGraw-Hill, 1983.

Baylick, M., and Saslow, L. *The Three Career Couple: Mastering the Fine Art of Juggling Work, Home, and Family*. Princeton, N.J.: Peterson's, 1993.

Berg, A. G. *How to Stop Fighting About Money and Make Some: A Couples' Guide to Personal Harmony and Financial Success*. New York: Avon Books, 1988.

Berg, B. J. *The Crisis of the Working Mother: Resolving the Conflict Between Family and Work*. New York: Summit Books, 1986.

Bingham, M., and Stryker, S. *More Choices: A Strategic Planning Guide for Mixing Career and Family*. Santa Barbara, Calif.: Advocacy Press, 1987.

Bodin, J., and Mitelman, B. *Mothers Who Work: Strategies for Coping*. New York: Ballantine Books, 1983.

Bravo, E. *The Job/Family Challenge: Not for Women Only*. New York: Wiley, 1995.

Bronfenbrenner, U. "What Do Families Do?" *Family Affairs* 4 (Winter–Spring 1991): 1–6.

Broverman, I. K., Broverman, D. M., Clarkson, F. E., Rosenkrantz, P. S., and Vogel, S. R. "Sex Role Stereotypes and Clinical Judgments of Mental Health." *Journal of Consulting and Clinical Psychology* 34 (1970): 1–7.

Canape, C. *The Part-Time Solution: The New Strategy for Managing Your Career While Managing Motherhood*. New York: Harper & Row, 1990.

Cardozo, A. R. *Sequencing: Having It All But Not All at Once . . . A New Solution for Women Who Want Marriage, Career, and Family*. New York: Atheneum, 1986.

Cowan, C. P., and Cowan, P. A. *When Partners Become Parents: The Big Life Change for Couples*. New York: Basic Books, 1992.

Crosby, F. J. *Juggling: The Unexpected Advantages of Balancing Career and Home for Women and Their Families*. New York: Free Press, 1991.

—— (ed.). *Spouse, Parent, Worker: On Gender and Multiple Roles*. New Haven, Conn.: Yale University Press, 1987.

Curley, J., Ladar, S., Siegler, A., Stevens, J. G., and Matthews, L. *The Balancing Act II: A Career and a Family: Five Women Reassess the Problems and Rewards*. Chicago: Chicago Review Press, 1981.

Dynerman, S. B., and Hayes, L. O. *The Best Jobs in America for Parents Who Want Careers and Time for Children Too*. New York: Rawson Associates, 1991.

Erikson, E. H. *Childhood and Society*, 2d ed. New York: W. W. Norton, 1993.

Family Resource Coalition. Special Focus: Work and Family. *Report* 11 (1992).

Fassel, D. *Working Ourselves to Death: The High Cost of Workaholism and the Rewards of Recovery*. San Francisco: HarperSan Francisco, 1990.

Feinstein, K. W. (ed.). *Working Women and Families*. Beverly Hills, Calif.: Sage, 1979.

Feldman, C. *Two Years Without Sleep: Working Moms Talk About Having a Baby and a Job*. Santa Barbara, Calif.: Blue Point Books, 1993.

Hall, F. S., and Hall, D. T. *The Two-Career Couple*. Reading, Mass.: Addison-Wesley, 1979.

Hanh, T. N. *Peace Is Every Step: The Path of Mindfulness in Everyday Life*. New York: Bantam Books, 1991.

Hendrix, H. *Getting the Love You Want: A Guide for Couples*. New York: Harper & Row, 1988.

Hewlett, S. A. *When the Bough Breaks: The High Cost of Neglecting Our Children*. New York: Basic Books, 1991.

Hochschild, A. *The Second Shift: Working Parents and the Revolution at Home*. New York: Avon Books, 1989.

Houston, V. *Making It Work: Practical Suggestions for Balancing the Needs of Your Career, Marriage, Children, and Self*. New York: Simon & Schuster, 1990.

Keyes, R. "Do You Have the Time?" *Parade Magazine*, February 16, 1992, pp. 22–25.

Kimbal, G. *The 50-50 Marriage*. Boston: Beacon Press, 1983.

Lerner, H. G. *The Dance of Anger*. New York: Harper & Row, 1985.

——. *The Dance of Intimacy*. New York: Harper & Row, 1989.

Lew, I. S. *You Can't Do It All: Ideas That Work for Mothers Who Work*. New York: Berkley Books, 1970.

Louv, R. *Childhood's Future: Listening to the American Family: New Hope for the Next Generation*. Boston: Houghton Mifflin, 1990.

Lowman, K. *Of Cradles and Careers: A Guide to Reshaping Your Job to Include a Baby in Your Life.* Franklin Park, Ill.: La Leche League International, 1984.

Magid, R. Y. *When Mothers and Fathers Work: Creative Strategies for Balancing Career and Family.* New York: AMACOM, 1987.

Mason, J. "Finding the Village in the City." *Mothering* 57 (1990): 105–109.

Mayer, G. G. *2001 Hints for Working Mothers.* New York: Quill, 1976.

McBride, K. *Tips for Working Parents: Creative Solutions to Everyday Problems.* Pownal, Vt.: Storey Communications, 1989.

Noble, B. P. "Now He's Stressed, She's Stressed." *New York Times,* October 9, 1994.

Olds, S. W. *Working Parents' Survival Guide.* Rocklin, Calif.: Prima Publishing & Communications, 1989.

Olmsted, B., and Smith, S. *Creating a Flexible Workplace,* 2d ed. New York: AMACOM, 1994.

———. *The Job Sharing Handbook.* San Francisco: New Ways to Work, 1996.

Pleck, J. *Working Wives/Working Husbands.* Beverly Hills, Calif.: Sage, 1985.

Rapoport, R., and Rapoport, R. *Dual-Career Families Re-Examined: New Integrations of Work and Family.* New York: Harper & Row, 1976.

Rose, K. *Program Models and Policies.* New York: John Wiley, 1993.

Saltzman, A. *Down-Shifting: Reinventing Success of a Slower Track.* New York: HarperCollins, 1991.

Sanger, S., and Kelly, J. *The Woman Who Works, The Parent Who Cares: A Revolutionary Program for Raising Your Child.* Boston: Little, Brown, 1987.

Scarf, M. *Intimate Partners: Patterns in Love and Marriage.* New York: Ballentine Books, 1987.

Schor, J. B. *The Overworked American: The Unexpected Decline of Leisure.* New York: Basic Books, 1991.

Shreve, A. *Remaking Motherhood: How Working Mothers Are Shaping Our Children's Future.* New York: Viking, 1987.

Sprankle, J. *Working It Out: The Domestic Double Standard.* New York: Walker & Co., 1986.

Stack, C. B. *All Our Kin: Strategies for Survival in a Black Community.* New York: Harper & Row, 1970.

Stelck, L., and Newman, C. *The Working Relationship: Management Strategies for Contemporary Couples.* New York: Villard Books, 1986.

Swiss, D. J., and Walker, J. P. *Women and the Work/Family Dilemma.* New York: Wiley, 1993.

Tannen, D. *You Just Don't Understand: Women and Men in Conversation.* New York: William Morrow, 1990.

Thomas, R. B. "Parenting and Professionalism: The Myth of Having It All." *Zero to Three* (December 1990): 13–17.

"The Value of Time." *Work Times* 9 (September 1991): 1.

VanWert, W. F. "The Transformation of a Single Father." *Mothering* 57 (1990): 29–33.

Weisberg, A. C., and Buckler, C. A. *Everything a Working Mother Needs to Know About Pregnancy Rights, Maternity Leave and Making Her Career Work for Her.* Garden City, N.Y.: Doubleday, 1994.

Wendkos-Olds, S. *Working Parents' Survival Guide.* Rocklin, Calif.: Prima Publishing & Communication, 1983.

Wolfson, R. M., and Deluca, V. *Couples With Children.* New York: Warner Books, 1982.

Zigler, E. F., and Lang, M. E. *Child Care Choices: Balancing the Needs of Children, Families, and Society.* New York: Free Press, 1991.

About the Authors

Deborah Lee, Ph.D. in social psychology, works with individuals, families, groups, and organizations. She is cofounder and former executive director of the Support Group Training Project, a nonprofit organization that trains people in initiating and facilitating peer support groups. Lee has done extensive writing on this subject, including three training manuals. She consults with varied organizations on family support and parenting issues.

Cary Martin Zellerbach, M.B.A., has been active in the investment field for nearly twenty years. Among her affiliations, she was a founding principal and executive vice president of Mellon Capital Management Corporation. She is currently associated with a private investment management firm. As a graduate of Wellesley College, she is a charter board member of the Wellesley Business Leadership Council. Zellerbach received her M.B.A. from Stanford Graduate School of Business, where she has served as trustee of the Stanford Business School Trust. She and her husband John are the parents of two elementary school children.

Chris Essex, M.A., is a parent educator in private practice and codirector of The Center for Work and the Family, in Berkeley, California. At the Center, Essex develops and coordinates parenting services, which include Noontime Parenting Groups at the Workplace, Preparation to Return to Work After Baby, Working Mother Support Groups, and Parenting Workshops and Consultation. She consults with the media on issues concerning working parents. She is the mother of a son.

Leah Potts Fisher, L.C.S.W., is a psychotherapist in private practice and codirector of The Center for Work and the Family. The Center provides support services for working men and women, both privately and in the workplace. Her interest in work/family integration grows out of more than twenty years of experience as a psychotherapist, marriage counselor, and group leader. She is particularly interested in the impact of work/family stress on couples' relationships. Fisher consults regularly with the media on issues regarding working parents. She is the mother of two teenagers.

Barney Olmsted is codirector and cofounder of New Ways to Work, a San Francisco-based resource development and research organization, where she consults, develops programs, and edits *Work Times,* the only national newsletter focused on flexible schedules in the workplace. Her book, *Creating a Flexible Workplace,* which she coauthored with Suzanne Smith, won the Society for Human Resources Management Award for the best book of 1990, and was revised in 1994. She is the mother of three grown children.

Index

The letter *n* after a page number indicates that the material is contained in a footnote.